What works in adoption and foster care?

Other titles in the series

What works in building resilience?

What works for children and young people with harmful sexual behaviours?

What works in leaving care?

What works for parents with learning disabilities?

What works in promoting the mental health of looked-after children?

What works in strategic partnership?

What works for troubled children?

What works in adoption and foster care?

Clive Sellick June Thoburn Terry Philpot

Published by Barnardo's

Tanners Lane

Barkingside

Ilford

Essex

IG6 1QG

Charity registration no 216250

First published 1996

Revised edition 2004

Designed and produced by Andrew Haig & Associates

Printed in the United Kingdom by Russell Press, Nottingham

A catalogue record for this book is available from the British Library

ISBN 1 904659 00 4

Contents

Case studies

About the authors

Clive Sellick is Senior Lecturer in Social Work, University of East Anglia. Before beginning his academic career he worked as a social worker and manager in various child and family social work settings. He has also served as a magistrate. He has researched and written widely in the field of foster care. He is the author and joint author or editor of four books and of several journal articles and book chapters. His current research interest centres on the policy and practice of the much-expanded independent fostering sector. He has also conducted a review of innovative fostering practice for the Social Care Institute for Excellence.

June Thoburn is Professor of Social Work, University of East Anglia. She has worked as a senior social worker in England and Canada and has been teaching and researching a wide range of child welfare topics since 1980. She has particular interests in family support services and in child placement. She frequently acts as an expert witness in complex childcare and adoption cases. One of her most widely read books is *Child placement: principle and practice* (1994a) and her most recent book (with Norford and Rashid) is *Permanent family placement for children of minority ethnic origin* (2000). She is a member of the General Social Care Council, and was awarded the CBE in 2002.

Terry Philpot is a writer on social policy and a regular contributor to several publications including *Times Higher Educational Supplement* and *The Tablet*. He was formerly editor and editor in chief of *Community Care*. He has written and edited several books, the latest of which are *Adoption: changing families, changing times* (with Anthony Douglas, 2003) and *Searching questions: identity, origins and adoption* (with Julia Feast, 2004). He has also published reports on kinship care and residential care for older people run by the Catholic Church. He is a member of the boards of the Centre for Policy on Ageing, Rainer and Social Care Institute for Excellence, and an associate of the Children and Families Research Unit, De Montfort University. He has won several awards for journalism.

Foreword

There can be few tasks more vital than caring for vulnerable children in ways that are well tested and evaluated. *What works in adoption and foster care?* was originally published by Barnardo's in 1996 as *What works in family placement?* by Clive Sellick and June Thoburn. With the support of the British Association for Adoption and Fostering, Barnardo's is delighted to be publishing this updated review of the research messages about this most important area of childcare practice.

This publication is particularly timely given the Department of Health's 'Choice Protects' review of fostering, and the commissioning and management of placement services. This book addresses many of the key objectives of that review. These focus on: the commissioning of high-quality services and packages of care and support for looked-after children; assessing need and involving children and carers; seeking well-evidenced models of commissioning and managing services which provide positive outcomes for children – through multi-agency commissioning and innovation; and the role and status of foster care, the recruitment and retention of carers, and support and training for carers.

Since 1996, the original 'What works?' publication has helped to guide many social work practitioners through complex decisions raised by the recruitment and training of foster carers and prospective adopters, matching children to carers and the maintenance and support of placements. A 2004 update of this book is timely – not least because Barnardo's continues to receive many requests for the original publication, and also because a great deal more has been published since 1996.

Through its 'What works?' series, Barnardo's aims to help practitioners to keep abreast of new research, make informed judgements about the strength of the evidence, sift old data from new research and to interpret the relevance of the findings to practice. We hope that you will find the 2004 edition and its new presentation both informative and accessible, a support to your practice and to your work with children in need of new family placements.

BAAF is very concerned to promote the importance of evidence-based practice, through its Research Advisory Group, annual symposiums and publications. It is sometimes the case that busy workers will base decisions about children's placements on established custom and practice – but as professionals we all owe it to children to be rigorous in reviewing the evidence base for our actions. This is why BAAF is delighted to be associated with this study.

Chris Hanvey
UK Director of Operations, Barnardo's

Felicity Collier
Chief Executive, British Association for
Adoption and Fostering

Acknowledgements

The authors of the first edition of this book were Clive Sellick and June Thoburn, and, with their detailed assistance, I have revised and updated much of the text for this new edition. The process also benefited from the help and guidance of Angela Hutton, Principal Officer (Research and Development) and Di McNeish, Director of Policy and Research, both of Barnardo's. Angela Hutton also collected the case studies with Kate Sugden, Research Assistant at Barnardo's.

This edition is also very much the product of the assistance, criticism and guidance of: Felicity Collier, Chief Executive, BAAF; Nick Dunster, Children's Services Manager, Barnardo's; Ann Frewin, Principal Practice and Policy Officer, Barnardo's; Mary Sainsbury, Project Manager, Practice Development Team, Social Care Institute for Excellence; and Pat Verity, freelance consultant. I thank the following for their help in locating research: John Simmonds, Director of Policy, Research and Development, BAAF; Robert Tapsfield, Chief Executive, Family Rights Group; Elizabeth Monck, Senior Research Officer, Thomas Coram Research Centre, University of London; and the staff of Barnardo's library.

I thank the following for information about Barnardo's projects: staff of RAFT (Residential and Families Together), Glasgow; staff of Genesis Family Placement Project Newcastle, and Breakaway, Dudley; Judith Matthews, Kath Sherwen and Mo O'Reilly, Children's Service Managers, New Families, Bradford, East Midlands Family Placement Service, Spondon and Jigsaw, Walthamstow, London, respectively; Cath Sartoris, Family Placements Manager, Leicestershire County Council; Peter Tomlin, Children's Services Manager, Fostering Adolescents in Merseyside (FAIM) and the young people who contributed to the discussion group at the FAIM discussion day; and staff and users of Midlands New Families, Halesowen.

Publication acknowledgements

The quotations from children and young people, adoptive parents and foster carers used in the text are taken from *Permanent family placement for children of minority ethnic origin* by Thoburn, Norford and Rashid, published in 2000 by Jessica Kingsley Publishers.

The sections on the recruitment, retention, assessment and training of foster carers and on placement decisions appear, in a slightly different form, in 'Family placement services' by Sellick and Thoburn in *What works for children?* edited by McNeish, Newman and Roberts, published in 2002 by the Open University Press.

The section on kinship care owes much to *Family problems, family solutions. Kinship care for children in need: agenda for change* by Philpot and Broad, published in 2003 by the Children and Families Research Unit, De Montfort University.

Terry Philpot

Introduction

Context for the second edition

Since the first edition of this book was published in 1996 as *What works in family placement?* (Sellick and Thoburn, 1996), there has been a growing interest in 'what works'. Evidence-based practice (to use another current term) had gained some government attention a while before this when, in 1994, Virginia Bottomley, then Secretary of State for Health, said: 'We need dramatically to improve our understanding of what works and what does not' (Sellick and Thoburn, 1996, p8). A new phase in the search for 'what works' began with the coming into being of the Social Care Institute for Excellence (SCIE) in October 2001, to collate, evaluate and disseminate evidence-based practice in social care.

During the intervening period, too, there has been a renewed interest by government in family placement. An early intimation of this occurred three years before the first edition of this book appeared, with the publication by the Conservative government of the White Paper on adoption (Department of Health, 1993). John Major had made known his own concerns about adoption, just as Tony Blair was to do. However, action on that subject was delayed until the new Labour government instituted the Prime Minister's review of adoption (Performance and Innovation Unit, 2000), which led to the White Paper (Department of Health, 2000) and the Adoption and Children Act, which received the Royal Assent at the end of 2002. A public service agreement target has been set for the numbers of children adopted from care to rise by at least 40 per cent – from about 2,700 in 2000 to about 4,000 in 2004/5.

Foster care has taken a back seat to adoption over the years, attracting far less public, media and political interest. One of the consequences of this has been the comparatively small amount of research into foster care. In recent years, however, numbers of children in foster care have grown due to the falling out of favour of residential care. In 2002 the Department of Health announced Choice Protects, a strategic review of foster care. The Welsh Assembly also gave notice of a similar review. SCIE contributed to Choice Protects by undertaking two projects: a practice review of innovative fostering schemes, and a research review examining the organisational arrangements that facilitate good outcomes in fostering.

Along with these changes, the Children (Leaving Care) Act 2000 placed new responsibilities on local authorities for children leaving their care, and Quality Protects set targets to reduce the average number of moves in any one year by looked-after children to ensure stability and promote attachment. This latter direction has been brought about by the evidence that many children in care experience multiple moves that prove disruptive to their emotional and psychological health, as well as their education.

Because every child has a right to expect that professionals intervening in their lives do so on the basis of the best available knowledge, it is incumbent on professionals and their employing agencies to be fully informed about those ways which are better than others at dealing with problems. But how are we to know which these are?

In his foreword to the first edition of this publication, Allan Currer, then Deputy Director of Child Care, Barnardo's, wrote:

> Those of us who provide services whose purpose is to support young children and their families were ourselves children once, and all of us can rightly claim some specialist knowledge of childhood. Equally, each of us will have clear ideas, based on our own childhood experience, our professional experience and perhaps our experience of parenthood, of 'what works' and what does not. How confident can we be that our interventions in children's lives are making a difference to the desired end? (Sellick and Thoburn, 1996, p5)

He went on to quote from a study commissioned by the Department of Health (Parker et al, 1991) which looked back to a time when much work to alleviate the harm done to children was based on a moral confidence and a belief in the extreme pliability of children once exposed to new environments separating them from bad influences. This view may be reflected in two contrasting aspects of past childcare. The first is the practice in adoption when children would often not be told that they were adopted because there was a belief that severing them from their 'bad' family for their new, adoptive and 'good' family was a surgical cut which would enable them to put their past behind them. Another policy from the past which reflected the idea of the beneficial effects of exposing children to new environments was that of child migration to Canada, New Zealand and Australia, which reached its height in the late nineteenth century but continued until the 1960s. Roy Parker and colleagues, who conducted the Department of Health research, put it thus: 'If what was being done in the interests of the child was self-evidently right the question of whether it actually led to desirable outcomes was hardly likely to be asked' (Parker et al, 1991, p1).

In modern social welfare and childcare, there ought not to be a conflict between values, which encompass a deep personal commitment by many workers, and evidence of what works. But we should not confuse values with value-judgements or judgements based on the best available evidence. We also need to exercise humility in recognising that what is absolutely 'known' to be right at one time will be 'known' to be wrong at another. In few areas does this apply more than in family placement. As Mike Fisher, Research Director of SCIE, has put it: 'It's not "what works" but "what works for whom and under what circumstances"' (quoted in Rickford, 2002).

When the first edition of this book was published in 1996, the authors suggested that some readers might feel that a drive to provide evidence-based welfare services to children was a diversion from the main task of offering help and support, or that this approach under-estimated the complexity of social work support. Since then, with the early debates about what evidence-based social work was really all about, and the creation of SCIE by Act of Parliament as a demonstration of the government's wish to seek value for money as well as effective services, such an apprehension may be all the greater. But how many of us, considering, for instance, medical treatment for our own children, would not want to know about success rates, risks, alternatives, if any, and what would happen if there was no intervention?

When it comes to children who need families, what are the questions that would occur to the prudent child, birth parent, social worker or adoptive parent? And does research help to provide the answer to such questions: Will this child be better off supported in his or her family of origin, or placed elsewhere? What percentage of permanent placements of children like this one (or children placed by this agency) 'work'? What are the long-term outcomes for children in adoption or long-term fostering placements? We make clear in this book that there is no dearth of well-conducted studies that address these very basic questions of longer-term outcomes, but also that there are many gaps in our knowledge.

There are, of course, difficult methodological issues in addressing outcomes for children but we believe that we probably under-use the best of what is already known, and place more emphasis than is wise on what is sometimes known in social work as 'practice wisdom'. Of course, those working with children and families over a long time will accumulate valuable experience, but only robust research will enable us to know how much of this experience is 'wisdom' and to disentangle, for instance, the successful record of a skilled practitioner from the practice methods employed, or the characteristics of the children placed.

There are many excellent descriptive studies in the field of child welfare that have contributed to the creation, development and replication of many sensitive, well-run services. However, there are fewer soundly based studies of effectiveness in actual practice and it is not always easy to trace those that do exist.

A word should be offered here about research into foster care. Until fairly recently (as recent, in fact, as when the first edition of this book first appeared) it was common to read about the paucity of such research (see, for example, Triseliotis et al, 1995 and Berridge, 1997). Indeed, Berridge makes a point of saying that when compiling his research review for the Department of Health he found only 13 detailed investigations of foster care in the UK in the previous two years but at the time that he was writing there were 10 major studies of residential care under way.

The irony is that fostering has been developed at the expense of residential care, which has been progressively in decline, in terms of placements available (and, indeed, in professional and public esteem) for a couple of decades. Thus, the largest research effort was being directed towards an increasingly rare placement option. By the same token, fostering was being expanded without much research evidence. Shaw and Hipgrave (1983) suggest why this should have been. They refer to the influence of Bowlby's work, especially arising from *Child care and the growth of love* (1953) and the discovery by local authority treasurers that fostering was cheaper. Together, as they put it, 'the blending of psychiatry and finance produced a heady brew' (p16).

However, since Berridge made his observation about research, the situation has now changed markedly. Several extensive studies have been undertaken across the UK in the past few years: Pithouse et al (1994) and Pithouse and Parry (1997) looked at the fostering services and structures of the eight then existing Welsh local social services authorities; Waterhouse (1997) examined fostering arrangements in 94 English local authorities; and Triseliotis and colleagues (2000) undertook a study of the 32 Scottish authorities. This latter report completed a comprehensive account of family placement studies in mainland Britain.

The much-enlarged (and enlarging) independent fostering sector has been studied by Clive Sellick (1999a), followed by the same author's national study with Connolly (Sellick and Connolly, 2001; 2002). Other recent studies include Aldgate and Bradley (1999), which explored the use of short-term and intermediate accommodation as a family support service to prevent long-term family breakdown. Sinclair and others (2000) examined over 500 foster placements in seven English local authorities. Schofield and colleagues (2000) and Schofield (2003), in a retrospective and the first stage of a longitudinal prospective study explored in depth the neglected research area of long-term foster care.

Lowe and colleagues (2002) have considered the factors that determine local authority decisions to pursue either adoption or long-term fostering. Thoburn, Norford and Rashid (2000) report on long-term outcomes for children of minority ethnic origin placed for adoption or with permanent foster families. Some recent research findings question established policy and practice, particularly regarding effective ways of recruiting and retaining foster carers.

Thus, after only seven years, a new edition of this book has been called for. For this new edition, it has been necessary to rewrite some sections of the text, and there has been some re-ordering of the content, as well as the addition of a substantial amount of new material. New research has been noted, in areas in which where there have been significant research advances. One topic, in particular, has been expanded – kinship care, much more prominent since 1996. However, while more has been written about kinship care, and the earliest research on its effectiveness dates from 1984, this is a field still under-researched. Reference is also made to concurrent planning, which is much newer to this country having been imported from the United States where it is more established but little researched.

What is offered here remains, as in 1996, an overview. It is not intended as a practice guide, and not as a textbook (although the most fundamental hope of the authors is that it will inform practice). Rather, it provides pointers and a basis for questions that practitioners will want to pose for themselves.

'Value for money' is a much-used phrase, and sometimes defined only vaguely, but it means that the purchasers and providers of services must ensure that services achieve their intended result with the resources that are available. Actions must be soundly informed so that they are effective. This applies to both statutory and voluntary agencies. Those who give to charity – individuals, churches or corporations – want to know that their money is well spent, and money from the public purse, too, must be properly spent. Most importantly, children and families using the services have a right to expect that practitioners and the state are acting on the basis of the best available knowledge.

The aims and approach of this book

There can be few more difficult or delicate decisions in social work than those taken with children and families. The effects of those decisions for many children may not be fully realised for many years and it may be difficult to distinguish between these interventions, other influences on the child and young person, and the effects of their growing to maturity.

The intention of this book, then, is to assist managers and practitioners in family and childcare social work to make decisions based on sound evidence about where to place children and what sort of practice is likely to bring about the desired outcomes for children, birth relatives, foster carers and the adoptive family.

Three specific questions are addressed.

- What does research indicate are the factors likely to be associated with positive outcomes?
- How can practice be evaluated and what outcome measures can be used?
- What does research *not* tell us, or where are the messages from research unclear or contradictory?

This book is not a research summary, and is not intended to compete with excellent research summaries that exist (Triseliotis, 1989; Bullock, 1990; Shaw, 1994; Berridge, 1996; Triseliotis et al, 1997; Department of Health, 1999). The first edition was written in consultation with Barnardo's staff (as this updated second edition has been) as a guide to what has been learned from research about what appears to work best in family placement. It is also intended to serve as a directory of some of the most important sources.

This is intended to be a practical, useful guide, with an anticipated readership among busy practitioners, as well as managers of services, to inform them about the findings of literature on research-based practice. The temptation is to say 'this does not apply to me' or 'we are doing that already'. However, it is often all too easy to regard research as relevant for only other people unless it focuses on the practitioner's own practice or agency. But to see research as something which is generally applicable – to be research-minded – means that we can learn from our own mistakes and successes but also from a much larger number of practitioners and types of practice. Such an attitude allows both objective insight and wider context.

The research, as will be seen, has many limitations but we hope to show that it also has many insights to offer the busy practitioner, which are relevant to not only how to practice but how to *evaluate* practice.

As the intended key reader is the busy practitioner, the book is structured to tie in with the tasks that make up family placement social work. These are:

- working with parents and children in the initial planning stages to decide whether placement is appropriate
- recruiting, assessing and training foster carers and adopters and developing their competence
- matching and placing children with foster and adoptive families
- encouraging comfortable contacts with family and others important to the child as appropriate
- providing supervision and support for carers and their families
- providing advice, guidance or therapy as appropriate to parents, children and carers
- helping children, parents and carers, where relevant, to plan for and move to independent living, or back home, or to another placement elsewhere.

The nature and content of these tasks will vary depending on the model of family placement and the characteristics of the children to be placed.

Some research covers the same ground and reaches similar conclusions. In this case, the most important studies are separately described and the key messages for different aspects of practice are then summarised, without necessarily referring to all the sources each time. (Some research, which appeared in the first edition, has been replaced by later, more up-to-date research.) We have also tried to indicate the strength of the evidence, to point out where researchers might disagree, and to say where the knowledge gaps are and where new research is urgently needed.

1 A spectrum of support: child placement research, theory and practice

Approaches to evaluating child placement

The task of evaluating child-placement practice is difficult because of the many discrete but interacting components of the effort to make any one placement successful. The efforts to be evaluated are those of a team of workers using different styles of practice at different times, and of the parents, the children and the carers themselves. Moreover, there are very many gaps in research-based knowledge on which to build child-placement practice. Many of the 'certainties' often cited are actually value statements about what should be done rather than what has been shown by research to be more effective.

Timescales are also important when trying to make sense of family placement research. It is easier to evaluate a short episode of care which has a clear purpose, such as a series of short breaks, or a single placement to hold a troubled adolescent in caring surroundings until a court hearing, than it is to evaluate all that happens when an abused 3-year-old is placed for adoption. Indeed, to put it at its simplest, the long-term outcomes for a child adopted as an infant may be measured 20 or more years after the placement, and the practice leading to these outcomes will have moved on in the intervening period.

We can evaluate casework intervention, perhaps a piece of behavioural work, if the child placed at age 3 starts to steal from his or her parents at the age of 8, in terms of whether the stealing then stopped. It is much harder to know whether caring and consistent parenting or skilled life-story work helped a child to turn the corner from being a withdrawn and unhappy 10-year-old to an averagely outgoing teenager. The more complex the placement circumstances, and the longer the timescale, the more difficult it is to attribute success to any one factor or type of placement.

The characteristics of the child needing placement will also have an impact on success rates. A 6-week-old baby may be placed before it has had too many damaging experiences. Teenagers are often on the move even in 'ordinary' families, and most studies of teenage placement schemes show quite high rates of breakdown. The larger the numbers in the study, the more these individual differences can be allowed for when considering the relationship between any one variable and outcome.

In larger-scale research studies where such factors can be controlled, it is possible to learn whether, in the majority of cases, a particular aspect of the service is associated with a successful outcome for a sub-group of children, such as emotionally disturbed 12-year-old boys, or infants who have Down's syndrome. (See the appendix by Sapsford in Fratter et al (1991), and Thoburn (1994b) for a fuller discussion of this question of controlling for the impact of one variable on another.) But only rarely are we able to say that it was a particular piece of work carried out in a certain way which was the cause of this (good or bad) long-term outcome for this particular child. And then, of course, there is the question of luck – a chance meeting with a more stable partner for the parent or for the teenager leaving care, or the commitment of a particular teacher or youth worker.

As Macdonald and Roberts point out when discussing research on 'what works' with families of younger children:

> In many cases, the most important outcomes of the interventions we make are not known for many years, and it may be difficult to distinguish the effects of our interventions from maturational effects –that is, children and young people change as they grow up. (Macdonald and Roberts, 1995, p6)

Two books that helpfully address the question of measuring outcomes in these more 'messy' situations are those by Cheetham and others (1992) and Parker and others (1991). Figure 1 gives an idea of how complex is the notion of outcome, and how difficult it is to be sure that a particular outcome is associated with a particular piece of practice. The large box illustrates the very many parenting activities that may have an impact on the outcome for the child and the smaller box shows the smaller but still substantial number of interventions by social workers or other professionals.

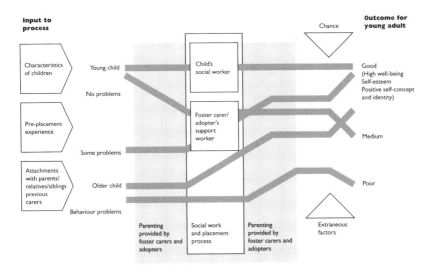

Figure 1 **The relationship between a child's experiences before placement, the placement process, parenting provided and outcome**

What is a 'successful' placement?

How might you recognise success or failure in your work? How do you measure 'success'? Indeed, what does success mean? This section includes several sets of 'outcome measures', giving examples of the results for clients and services which have been used in child-placement research. There is not much that individual placement workers can do about evaluating the long-term outcome of their day-to-day practice, even if they stay around in the same area for years and do what Barbara Kahan (1979) and Pamela Mann (1984) did and track down and interview children who were on their caseloads years before. However, our knowledge about the characteristics of the child's life and day-to-day parenting which appear to be associated with good outcomes make it possible to consider *interim* outcome measures.

Whether or not they have a sense of permanence and a sense of personal identity as they grow up are particularly useful interim outcome measures for children in place-ment, but they need to be put alongside the other measures which developmental psychology research indicates are important for all children. The Looking After Children Assessment and Action Records (Parker et al, 1991; Ward, 1995) are based on this research on the impact of parenting and child development.

Following the work of Parker and others (1991) and Ward (1995) on interim outcome measures, the Department of Health funded work to develop a set of schedules to be used to measure whether the day-to-day needs of looked-after children are met. Evidence from longitudinal studies suggests that if success is achieved using these interim measures, the long-term outcomes are more likely to be positive. The development of these Looking After Children Assessment and Action Records is described by Ward (1995), and a particularly interesting chapter describes how 'ordinary families' measure up. These measures are now being developed further, for use with all children in need and their parents and carers, as part of the Department of Health's Integrated Service Framework.

The assessment indicators for looked-after children are:

- health, including physical and mental health
- education
- identity, including ethnic and cultural identity
- family and social relationships
- social presentation
- emotional and behavioural development
- being able to care for themselves.

On several measures, including the consumption of a healthy diet, and help with homework, looked-after children on average receive parenting which is the same or better than that experienced by those living in families from similar backgrounds, as also found by Jane Aldgate and colleagues (1992). Many local authorities are now integrating this system for detailed monitoring of the needs of children into reviewing practice (Bailey et al, 2002). For the moment they are essentially practice tools, but work is being undertaken to adapt them for evaluative purposes so that a worker or a team of workers may use them to evaluate the progress of a particular child over time, or in combination to look at the success of the whole team in meeting the needs of children in placement. These measures can help researchers and practitioners to monitor more routine aspects of children's lives, such as their health, social competence and relationships with relatives and with peers.

In the past, researchers have tended to concentrate on negative aspects of the placement such as disturbed behaviour and difficulties in behaviour, or indeed whether or not the placement broke down, rather than considering whether the child is meeting developmental milestones and receiving the sort of parenting which is most likely to achieve steady growth and development.

Another further important measure of outcome is the level of satisfaction felt by adults and children with the work undertaken and with the placement itself. People are more likely to persist in a placement when they have a sense of satisfaction and fulfilment. The research cited later in this book tells us that, when there is this sense of satisfaction, the children placed frequently emerge at the other end as averagely emotionally healthy people. Subjective views on outcome are therefore extremely important, at least in the interim stages. However, it is possible to be over-reliant on satisfaction or consumer studies, which are frequently subject to varying degrees of bias.

Measures of outcomes for children and parents

'Well-being' is often used as an aggregate measure of outcome, and may be, for example, the well-being in the interim or long-term, for the child, parents, relatives, foster carers, new parents or siblings in a new family. Scoring well on psychological tests of emotional and/or mental health or self-concept may be evidence of this, and included is the extent to which the child is protected and kept safe from harm by the carers or others. (Two high-profile cases in 2002 of children being murdered by their foster and adoptive parents have acted as reminders of the importance of safety as an outcome measure.)

Another aggregate measure is the extent to which a young person has a positive sense of himself or herself as a person of the particular ethnic, cultural or religious group to which he or she belongs. This is very difficult to measure, however, other than by self-reporting.

Some more specific measures of success in a placement, include, for a young person:

- a realistic sense of identity based on accurate knowledge of origins and early life
- exams passed as appropriate to ability
- regular employment
- no criminal record, and no misuse of drugs or alcohol
- no experience of serious mental illness
- growing up 'attached' to at least one adult in a parenting role
- on reaching adulthood, making and maintaining a positive relationship with those of his or her own age, a partner and any children
- having a secure place within a 'family for life'
- no emotional ill effects from the adoption or fostering experience.

Measures of successful outcomes for parents or siblings include:

* adoptive parents or foster carers not suffering stress-related ill health
* relationships with partners being unimpaired by the placement
* birth parents' well-being not being significantly harmed by the placement of the child
* birth parents' children (siblings and half-siblings of the child placed) not being significantly harmed by the placement of their brother or sister.

'Satisfaction' is a measure of outcome that can be applied to any aspect of the work – the casework service, the training provided, or the placement service as a whole. Examples of interim and long-term satisfaction include:

* children's satisfaction with the parenting they received
* the adopters' or foster carers' assessment of the rewards from taking the child into their home, compared with what they anticipated when they applied to foster or adopt
* the birth parents' assessment of what was achieved by the placement of the child, compared with what they hoped for.

Ways of measuring service outcomes

* What proportion of children with a learning disability received short-break care, when their parents requested it?
* What proportion of placements for adoption broke down in a given timescale?
* What proportion of adopters experiencing difficulties in parenting a child received an adoption support service for themselves, for the children or for the family as a whole?
* What proportion of parents whose children returned home from long-term foster care had an agreement about the type of support services to be provided?
* Did children whose short-term and intermediate foster carers were regularly visited by a support worker experience fewer changes of placement than those whose carers did not receive this support?
* Does the child maintain comfortable contact with parents, siblings and school friends?
* What proportion of children received regular statutory visits and reviews?
* What proportion of foster carers attended regular post-approval training sessions?
* Did foster carers receive payments, support, placement contracts and out-of-hours support services?

Service outcome measures make assumptions, mostly based on client outcome research, that the service provided is beneficial. If service outcome measures are used, they should always be linked with evidence that the particular service is more likely than not to be of benefit to those who use it. There is, for example, evidence that children who experience an adoption breakdown in their early teens are likely to be worse off as young adults than those who remain with their adopters. There is evidence that children and young people who are adopted tend to do better when they have comfortable contact with birth parents and siblings.

Questions of cost should be included in service outcome measures, since cheaper services providing the same benefit free up resources to fill service gaps. But this may raise the question of at whose expense is the service being provided cheaply. Similarly, an expensive service that has clear benefits may prove to be better value for money than cheaper but unverified interventions.

Types of studies used in research on child placement

Despite the length of our bibliography, there is very little research in the UK on how children fare in short-term and intermediate foster placement, and not all that much more on what happens to them in permanent placement. Some of the earlier studies combined the two and tend not to be specific about the nature of the placement practice, the problems and characteristics of the children or the characteristics of the carers. Therefore the variables associated with the placement can rarely be linked to outcome. When they are (as with Berridge and Cleaver, 1987) the numbers are frequently too small to generalise from the findings.

In short, large-scale studies or surveys usually lack detail about service inputs; small-scale studies have the detail, but the numbers are too small and the research design may be inadequate for any predictive or causative inferences to be drawn from them.

However, some key studies of single agencies or groups of agencies give pointers about what appears to be associated with better outcomes, and most of these describe the practice in some detail. Examples of such studies include: Berridge and Cleaver (1987) and Cliffe and Berridge (1991) on different types of foster care; Trent (1989) and Farmer and Parker (1991) on helping children to return home; or Thoburn and colleagues (1986), Thoburn (1990) and Borland and others (1991) on permanent family placement work in voluntary and statutory agencies; Lowe and Murch with others (2002) on factors which determine the choice of adoption or long-term fostering.

Broadly, the research can be divided into longitudinal studies, following a group of children over time, and snapshot studies focusing on a single time period. There are very few randomised controlled trials or quasi-experimental design studies which use control groups to compare outcomes of services, although some North American studies exist (Stein at al, 1978; Jones, 1985). Less rare, but still infrequent, are quasi-experimental designs using comparison groups such as that of Gibbons and others (1995) which compared abused children who remained at home or were adopted or fostered with a comparison group of 'non-abused' children in similar communities.

More frequently, researchers compare groups of clients receiving different types of services: the services are described and the outcomes measured (for example, Lahti's study (1982) of different sorts of permanent placement work in the USA). Studies more often follow cohorts of children, consider the outcomes, and seek to link the different outcomes to the different features of the children, carers and the service received (for example, Berridge and Cleaver, 1987; Thoburn and Rowe, 1991). Other writers, mainly of in-house reports, make assumptions based on their own clinical experience about what seems to work and describe their practice. Many of the early studies come into this group.

When considering research findings it is important to assess the strength and reliability of the evidence presented. For example, research based on experimental designs, particularly if the findings have been replicated, provides a high degree of validity. Descriptive studies of practice, while illuminating, need to be treated with caution when considering outcomes. Examples of types of study are provided here, but are described in more detail in the relevant sections.

Prospective longitudinal studies

Prospective longitudinal studies identify a group of children and follow them for a period of years. The Department of Health's *Annual report of children looked after* is the major source of cross-sectional data on children looked after by local authorities and has been developed to allow for individual children's care careers to be followed.

The best-known UK longitudinal survey, in which some sub-samples have focused specifically on children placed away from home, is the National Child Development Study. It concerns a group of 17,000 children born in 1958 who have been followed up at regular intervals, the most recent follow-up being when the members of the group were 35. They included children who were adopted, and others who were fostered at some stage though numbers are relatively small and much of the detail about the contributions of service is limited.

Another example of this kind of study is Bohman and Sigvardsson's study (1980) of Swedish adoptions. Other detailed longitudinal prospective studies are those of Tizard (1977) and Tizard and Hodges (1990) on adoption of children placed from institutions, while Thoburn and colleagues (1986) and Thoburn (1990) looked at 29 children referred to one agency for permanent family placement. Millham and colleagues (1986) and Bullock and colleagues (1993) followed a group of 450 children entering local authority care (and most of whom were placed at some time in foster care) for ten years or until they returned home. Within this larger group, qualitative methods were used to study 30 families in more detail for the first two years.

Retrospective longitudinal studies

These studies take groups of children at a particular time, consider how well they are doing then, and look backwards to see what happened to them in the past and which characteristics may be associated with different outcomes. The problem with looking back is that the information about the influences, the prior characteristics of the children and the nature of past practice is often not available in the detail required. Sometimes 'retrospective' studies are linked with earlier 'prospective' studies to diminish these problems, such as one important study of parenting competence of mothers who had been in care (Rutter et al, 1983). Gibbons and colleagues' (1995) retrospective study of abused children eight years after protective intervention builds on the National Society for the Prevention of Cruelty to Children register studies, which collected basic data on all registered children at the time of registration.

Some researchers (for example, Nelson, 1985; Festinger, 1983; Thoburn and Rowe, 1991; Charles et al, 1992) collect a group of children already placed and then both look back at what has happened and follow up the children prospectively. Berridge and Cleaver's 1987 study of foster-home breakdown is an example of a more detailed quantitative and qualitative retrospective study, as is that of Farmer and Parker (1991) of children going home on trial. Joan Fratter's account (1996) of open adoptions is based on a non-random sample of in-depth interviews with parents, adopters, and children drawn mainly from Thoburn and Rowe's (1991) longitudinal retrospective survey. The adoptive parents in 22 families were interviewed several years after the placement and again four years later.

Snapshot studies

Snapshot studies tend to describe a group of children being looked after, and share some of the characteristics of retrospective studies in that they tend to look back to see what has happened in the past to help to interpret the present. Examples of such studies are Rowe and colleagues (1984) on long-term foster care; Stone (1995) on short-term foster care; and the survey by Rowe and colleagues (1989) of placements being made and children currently looked after during a particular year. These snapshot studies may examine large groups of children through casework records or questionnaires completed by social workers. Some, including the major study by Rowe and colleagues (1989) of over 10,000 placements, follow up the children usually for a period of one or two years. Smaller and more detailed studies, such as that of Sellick (1992) on the support of short-term foster carers, use non-random samples but can provide more detail because of the depth of the interviews. Some combine cohort studies with a small number of in-depth non-random interviews (for example, Rowe and colleagues (1984) which also included a video of birth parents talking of their experiences of the long-term care of their children).

Descriptive accounts of practice

These can be accounts by practitioners describing their own practice, or by researchers invited to observe and describe practice, often of a single agency. Many of the accounts of recruitment and training of foster carers come into this category. They are helpful when new ways of working are being developed, as with the *Practice Papers* written by Parents for Children (Sawbridge, 1983) or the short pamphlets of the workers at the London Post-Adoption Centre. Their value is increased if they are linked with evaluative research studies, as is the case with the Post-Adoption Centre as evaluated by Howe and Hinings (1989).

Single-case design or 'biographical' accounts

There are few 'pure' single-case design accounts (where inputs and outputs are carefully recorded) by family placement researchers. Such accounts as there are tend to be found in the professional journals, and overlap with descriptive studies. The biographical and autobiographical accounts by carers, young adults placed as children and birth parents (for example, Argent, 1988; Ryburn, 1994b; Phillips and McWilliams, 1996) or social workers (for example, Kahan, 1979; Mann, 1984) come loosely into this category. Some books combine several accounts.

Value-based literature

This is not research literature but may be based on research or clinical practice and seeks to influence policy and practice. Much of the writing on same-race placement comes into this category, as practitioners and agencies put together what little is known from research in order to support a form of practice which accords with social-work values. The pamphlet by Berridge and Smith (1993) on the placement of black children comes into this category.

Effective work with children and families

Child placement is an integral part of child and family social work practice. The success or otherwise of the child placement worker depends in part on the quality of the interventions in the life of the child and parents before and after placement. The success of work with one member of the placement 'triangle', the child for example, will be influenced by the quality of the work with the members of the birth family and with the carers or adopters.

In the rest of this chapter, we concentrate on what is known about effective child and family social work more generally, before moving on specifically to look at short-term and intermediate placement work (Chapter 2), and then at permanent placement work (Chapter 3).

The characteristics of a child at the time of placement will have a major impact on his or her long-term well-being (see Figure 1, above). The aim of the placement service is to attempt to improve the child's physical, intellectual and emotional well-being, and to address any unhelpful behaviour patterns as he or she grows up. Even if serious harm has already occurred, the provision of high-quality day-to-day parenting, and if possible the maintaining or forming of new bonds of affection, is likely to give the young person a reasonable chance of making more satisfactory relationships in adult life.

In most cases, help will take the form of providing support (including short-break care) to birth parents and their children, or helping parents and adolescents to get on better together. A smaller number of children, however, need either new parents or carers who can supplement parental care for a longer period. Thus, when evaluating placement services, as detailed below, we are considering:

- the parenting work of the carers themselves – the quality of the care they offer
- the casework and case-management services provided by the social workers for

the children and birth relatives, and by the family placement workers
- the decisions made about placement.

Although researchers try to disentangle these variables it can never be entirely clear that any positive or negative outcome results from one aspect of the service rather than another.

The parenting task

Several researchers have examined variables associated with the task of parenting: Colton (1988), Rushton and Treseder (1986), Rushton et al (1995), Tizard (1977), Tizard and Hodges (1990), Quinton et al (1998), and those monitoring the Looking After Children materials (Ward, 1995). Colton (1988) concluded that foster carers were more able to meet children's needs than residential workers of similar competence because a foster care setting enabled a more flexible and child-oriented approach. The role of carers in helping children to fulfil their potential at school has also been studied (Aldgate et al, 1992).

Studies that include the views of carers, birth parents and young people also tend to concentrate on aspects of parenting, as with the Who Cares studies conducted by Fletcher (1993) and Timms and Thoburn (2003). Most researchers describe parenting but some, such as Rushton and colleagues (1995), have attempted to find a way of describing *and evaluating* the parenting provided by new parents, and using it as a variable related to outcome. Most researchers have looked at fostering or adoptive-parenting variables in terms of biography (age, marital status, family size, ethnicity), values, motivation, or personality characteristics such as determination or sense of humour.

Research specifically on supplementary and substitute parenting will be returned to in more detail in the following chapters. The terms 'supplementary' and 'substitute' family care are often used in the professional literature, rather than 'short-term and intermediate' and 'long-term' foster care, or temporary and permanent family care. Supplementary foster care is generally a short-term or intermediate service for families and children to assist them in overcoming a temporary crisis or medium-term problems. Substitute family placement implies a longer period of care for children separated from parents who are either unable or unwilling to provide a home for their children until adulthood. These children need substitute parents, although their birth parents may continue to play some part in their lives.

The social work service: casework and therapy

Millions of words have been written about social work theory and practice, and evaluations have taken up many volumes. To simplify this large volume of work, we look here at three aspects of child placement practice. We consider the main contributions using the language of social casework – a term which best describes the many different contacts between the social worker, the different family members, and the carers, and which are all intended to support, advise and help, sometimes also offering therapy to achieve change. In *Child placement: principles and practice* (Thoburn, 1994a) this is divided into relationship, deeds or services, and words or therapy.

Sometimes caseworkers undertake the work themselves, and sometimes they are responsible for ensuring that it is done by someone else. This notion of social casework incorporates the social-care planning and counselling roles (described by the Barclay committee (1982) on the roles and tasks of social workers) or the 'purchaser' or 'care manager' and 'provider' roles now characteristic of local authority social work with adults, since the NHS and Community Care Act 1990. The work may be undertaken by someone who is a key worker or care manager, or by a team within a family centre or family resource unit.

Because of the complexity of the social casework role and tasks, researchers usually choose to evaluate one small aspect of it, perhaps a casework method such as task-centred casework or behavioural casework. The difficulty then is that the whole may be greater than the sum of the parts. Two workers may be using task-centred methods in similar cases but one may be more successful than the other because of the nature of the casework relationship that they are able to form rather than the particular techniques they are using. Howe (1994) summarised research indicating that relationship – including accurate empathy, warmth and genuineness – is central to effective helping. These principles or qualities were articulated most famously in Biestek's classic text (1961).

But child placement work is complex and so it is more difficult to relate these qualities to more complex and comprehensive measures of success, such as the survival of a placement that might otherwise have broken down, or the young adult's sense of self-worth. Research which has evaluated specific methods or interventions in terms of whether they are associated with specific changes of behaviour has produced evidence that task-centred and other clearly defined methods of intervention are more successful in achieving change than are longer-term, relationship-based methods.

However, in applying this body of research to child and family social work practice, including child placement, it needs to be considered that problems experienced by families needing such intervention are frequently complex and connected with a range of other difficulties, and most work tends to go on for periods of years rather than weeks. Consumer studies make it very clear that all kinds of families value a dependable relationship with a worker who cares about them. For example, this is found with original families (Packman et al, 1986; Fisher et al, 1986); foster carers (Sellick, 1992); and new families (Thoburn et al, 1986; Sellick, 1999b; Fisher et al, 2000).

It may be possible to combine these messages by thinking of effective practice in terms of short-term interventions (such as a short period of marital counselling for adoptive parents whose marriage is under stress) within the context of a long-term, helping relationship. Thus, if a child or a parent talks about suicidal impulses, or a behavioural problem is having a very negative impact on sibling relationships, a brief focused piece of work may be undertaken by either the social worker or a therapist brought in specifically to work on this particular problem, but the long-term relationship-based work is continued in the background.

Although research shows that over a period of years a child looked after by the local authority will experience changes of worker, most studies have shown that some child and family care workers have been in the same post for several years. However, in certain parts of the country – most notably London – there is so severe a shortage of social work staff that childcare services would be in danger of collapse were it not for the employment of agency staff.

It is important to recognise the very wide range of families using child placement services. Some will have pressing practical problems that will be alleviated by the provision of a short-break care service, but will also have the emotional resilience and the family and neighbourhood supports that make the provision of a relationship-based social casework service unnecessary. Short-term work may be needed to help the child to cope with the start of a regular period of planned short-break care, but it is most likely that the parent and the carers, with the support and advice of the social worker, will undertake this.

Next along the continuum come those families who have relationship or emotional problems as well as the need for practical help, and short-break care. Their needs for therapy or emotional support may, however, be short-term and intermediate and in response to a particular event such as a death in the family or marriage breakdown.

For them, short-term relationship-based counselling or a brief task-centred casework service may be all that is needed.

For the majority of families needing child-placement services, the problems are more deep-seated, and sometimes require services lasting for a period of years. The studies reported in the Department of Health research reviews *Social work decisions in child care* (Department of Health and Social Security, 1985) and *Patterns and outcomes in child placement* (Department of Health, 1991b) and the more recent *The Children Act now: messages from research* (Department of Health, 2001b) indicate that satisfaction of parents and children is related to the provision of a service which is purposive, provides appropriate practical help and advice, and is delivered in the context of a caring and dependable relationship.

Most of these studies have consumer satisfaction as their outcome measure, but an American study by Jones (1985) did use more objective measures of outcome, including whether or not services appeared to reduce the need for out-of-home placement and whether or not the children needed to stay in placement or were able to return home. Maluccio and colleagues (2000) summarise outcome research on family social work in the UK, USA and Australia.

In the British context, family centres are particularly appropriate places for the provision of this sort of service. The partnership principle embodied in the Children Act 1989 is an essential part of such a model in that it gives power to the families to make decisions about whether they wish to leave or re-enter the services provided, and includes the notion of help being a resource to the family. Maluccio and colleagues in the USA have researched family-support and family-placement services, and take the argument further in terms of partnership and competence-based models of family support, which include placement as a source of support for families:

> Parents need to be asked if they are satisfied with the way things are progressing. Are there services they would like to change? Is there a different kind of help they would like? (Maluccio et al, 1986, p146)

Consumer views reported by researchers in the UK and America suggest that parents, older children and carers should have a major say in the social work methods which are used to help them, rather than the decisions being entirely agency-led. This is a pertinent point since there has been a tendency in the UK, as well as in the USA, for service agencies to move from one fashionable method to the next, leaving little choice to families about the method they would find most helpful, and providing little information to service users on the relative effectiveness of methods.

Evaluating child placement work is even more complex when different service users disagree about desired outcomes, let alone how to achieve them. Research and Social Services Inspectorate reports (Department of Health, 1995a; Lambert et al, 1990; Millham et al, 1986; 1989) and the work of post-adoption centres indicate that few agencies have found a way to consult and involve birth parents whose views conflict with those of an agency.

The social work service: case management

Foster care is just one of a range of services which may make up a package of support for a family, and is most successful when provided in combination with other forms of care before, during and after placement. Practical services such as day care and welfare-rights advice receive the highest ratings of satisfaction from service users. Volunteer visiting schemes have been evaluated more frequently than other practical services. Generally, they are well received by family members but most of the studies have concentrated on rates of satisfaction rather than objective outcome measures of the progress made by children and parents. The first book in the series of Barnardo's 'What works?' publications looked at services to younger children living with their families (Macdonald and Roberts, 1995).

To conclude this section on the effectiveness of general family social work that forms the backdrop to child-placement work, it appears that the reappraisal of John Bowlby's work in the 1960s and 1970s, suggesting that early harm to children was likely to be reversed by the provision of good parenting, may have been over-optimistic. Recent studies of children receiving good care in permanent family placements who continued to show serious signs of disturbance, including poor attachments, suggest that although early harm may be reversible, there is a risk that it will not be totally reversed and that symptoms of disturbance will persist into adulthood.

This is an important reminder of the dangers of short-term thinking. It may be possible through a period of brief intervention to change the behaviour of parents, but it appears to be more difficult to reverse the harmful effects of early adverse experiences on the children themselves. Long-term, albeit episodic, therapy is likely to be needed by children who have suffered early harm, wherever they are placed. This message from an early study of the consequences of child abuse (Lynch and Roberts,

1982) has been reinforced by more recent studies. In one of the studies reported in *Child protection: messages from research* (Dartington Social Research Unit, 1995), Gibbons and others (1995) report on an evaluation of children eight years after they were physically abused or severely neglected when under the age of 5. They found that on average their well-being was lower than that of a matched sample of children who had not been abused, and that there was little difference among the abused children between those who had remained at, or returned, home and those who had been placed in foster or adoptive families. Thus, it cannot be assumed that, when the abuse has stopped and adequate parenting is provided, early harm will be reversed.

Making decisions about placement

The final major aspect of practice in child placement to be evaluated is the decision-making process and the effects of the different decisions. The key decisions are:

- whether to provide a placement for the child
- the length of the placement
- whether residential care, boarding education, foster family or kinship care should be used
- whether the placement should be voluntary or compulsory
- what sort of contact with members of the first family or previous carers, and with which ones, should be facilitated (or this may be one of the very small number of cases where even indirect contact with any member of the first family is inappropriate)
- whether financial help and practical support should be offered to the birth family or carer family
- the nature of any casework or therapeutic services to be provided to a child, parents or carers to support the placement.

Back to the spectrum of support

To assess what is known about the effectiveness of the different aspects of child-placement practice, the next two chapters of this book look separately at: short-term and intermediate foster care (Chapter 2); and permanent family-placement work (chapter 3). However, a comprehensive placement service must consider how the two forms of placement interact. Short-term and intermediate placement workers must always be aware that the work they do will make a profound difference to the possibility of achieving permanence for the child, whether this is achieved through placement home with the birth family or relatives, or by placement with a permanent new family, or in some form of group care.

It has become increasingly apparent that the theory and practice of short-term and intermediate foster care was neglected in the 1980s in the pursuit of 'permanence policies', and that without effective short-term and intermediate foster care the attempts to provide permanence for children have been severely impeded. Unnecessary moves for children within the care system, which were frequently unplanned, have made the task of permanent placement far more difficult than it need have been (Berridge and Cleaver, 1987). Foster care research and practice in Europe reinforces the view that, leaving aside special schemes for teenagers or children with disabilities, foster care has been undervalued, and theory and practice have remained relatively under-developed in Britain compared other parts of Europe.

The research studies to which we refer throughout this book come from all the traditions we have described in this chapter. All the studies included (and some of those which we have left out because there were more recent or more comprehensive studies on the same topic) have validity in their own terms. Practitioners can learn something from each of them. However, when it comes to using research to throw light on specific decisions to be made about specific children, there is no alternative to a careful scrutiny of the studies that seem most relevant. An appraisal must then be made as to the validity of their conclusions in the context of the specific case.

Key messages from research on the effectiveness of child placement

- Child placement is an integral part of child and family social work. It is important to consider outcomes of child placement in the context of practice with families and children generally.
- Outcomes for children are subject to many complex and interacting variables. The more complex the placement circumstances, the more difficult it is to attribute success to any one factor or type of placement.
- Timescales are important, and the measurement of long-term outcomes is particularly challenging.
- There are a number of outcome measures applied by researchers, which can provide important information for practice.
- When considering research findings it is important to assess the strength and

reliability of the evidence presented, and whether the research method used is appropriate to the question being studied.

- Both birth families and new families value a dependable relationship with a worker who cares about them.
- Effective practice, therefore, combines short-term and intermediate interventions within the context of long-term helping relationships.

2 **What works in short-term and intermediate foster care?**

This chapter encompasses a very wide range of practice. At one end of the spectrum, some short-break care schemes merge with family support schemes. At the other end, there is an overlap between professional fostering schemes and residential care, including therapeutic group care.

We first summarise the main studies that examine and evaluate the framework of short-term and intermediate foster care in the UK, Scandinavia and North America, including Canada. They include research studies on: short-break care for families where there is a disabled member as well as those at risk of long-term family break-down; studies of short-term and intermediate foster care for children whose families are in crisis and where assessments may result in them either returning home or moving on to other families; and specialist or treatment foster care schemes often for older children and young people.

Roger Bullock comments on the implications for how each of these foster care schemes requires different approaches to the recruitment and retention of foster carers. He writes:

> Foster care, which is the main alternative to care by the child's own family, has to fulfil a wide range of tasks and functions. These vary from nurturing an abandoned baby or containing a serious offender to the temporary care of a child whose mother is having another baby. Foster care, therefore, is not a single approach and its variety needs to be acknowledged in the recruitment, training and support of foster carers. (Bullock, 1990: 43)

The wider world of childcare practice and research has always influenced fostering practice, and research in foster care has had an important impact on child and family social work. The emphasis in the Children Act 1989 on the accommodation of children as a family support service and not as a sign of failure has its roots in the Department of Health studies of child placement summarised in *Social work decisions in child care* (Department of Health and Social Security, 1985) and *Patterns and outcomes in child placement* (Department of Health, 1991b).

Similarly, the encouragement by the Children Act of contact between fostered children and their birth families is another example since the research on cohorts of placed children concluded that comfortable contact is associated with a greater likelihood of children being reunited with their families and neighbourhoods (Aldgate, 1980; Fisher et al, 1986; Millham et al, 1986; Farmer and Parker, 1991; Bullock et al, 1993).

Accommodation, contact and reunification have a fundamental impact on contemporary foster care policy and practice. They influence the content of information and recruitment campaigns; the values, knowledge and skills underpinning foster carer training; the ingredients of assessment and approval programmes; and the methods of support for foster carers. These themes impinge on the tasks of even very temporary foster care. The particular emphasis may change, but a young child needing care away from home while a parent has a brief spell in hospital, or a teenager needing help to keep out of trouble while remanded in foster care both require high-quality and individualised personal care as well as help to remain in touch with their families and neighbourhoods.

The extent and nature of short-term and intermediate foster care in the UK

The experiences of children and young people in care

'When I was at the other school, being fostered was like a blight – was like a mark on your record. It was held against you, it was more like something that was held against you if you were fostered. I call the foster parents mum and dad but I was always the foster kid. The reason I say this is because at the end of the day, they didn't treat me like they treated their own son. They treated him better without a doubt.'
FOSTERED YOUNG PERSON WHOSE PLACEMENT WAS DISRUPTED

'There are times when I feel adopted and that I don't belong.'
ADOPTED YOUNG PERSON

'People know that I'm fostered. It's nothing to be ashamed of. Questions tend to come up when I'm out with Stewart and Mary [white foster carers]. For me, fostering was the best thing that ever happened. It might not be the best thing for another child.'
TRANSRACIALLY FOSTERED YOUNG PERSON

'I don't really tell anybody that I am fostered. When I talk to people about Annie, it's easier to refer to her as my aunty. They know she is not my mum. When I was little I was teased

about being fostered and they used to think that we were adopted. They didn't really understand. They treated us like we had some disease.'
FOSTERED CHILD

'Being a social worker is a treacherous job. You either have it or you don't. There's no tips I can give. Social workers need to be able to read between the lines and observe young people because they may not tell them everything. That is what I am saying. You can't teach this sort of thing. Social workers have it or they don't. My social worker didn't, or if she did, she didn't give a damn.'
YOUNG MAN, 20, WHOSE PLACEMENT BROKE DOWN

In 2001 around 75,000 children and young people were looked after by local authorities across the UK (National Statistics Office, 2001). Of these children, 77 per cent live in England, 3 per cent in Northern Ireland, 14 per cent in Scotland and 5 per cent in Wales (Department of Health 2002; Department of Health, Social Services and Public Safety, 2001; Scottish Executive, 2002; National Assembly for Wales, 2002).

Looked-after children are cared for in a variety of settings, the most common being foster care, residential accommodation and pre-adoptive placements. However, placement patterns differ across the UK. Some children are in care under care orders but are placed with their parents. In England, Northern Ireland and Wales, over 60 per cent of looked-after children are in foster care whereas in Scotland this figure is 28 per cent (and 65 per cent in England, 63 per cent in Northern Ireland, 74 per cent in Wales.)

Children living with their parents under supervision are included in the statistics on looked-after children. In Scotland, 45 per cent of children included in the looked-after statistics are cared for by parents under supervision, while in Northern Ireland 20 per cent of children on care orders are placed with parents. In England and Wales the corresponding figure is only 11 per cent. The higher figure for Scotland is partly because young offenders are included within the statistics for children and young people looked after and supervised at home.

Across the UK, 10,000 looked-after children and young people live in some form of residential home or secure unit. As a result of the high number of foster placements, fewer children in Wales (6 per cent), compared to the rest of the UK, live in residential accommodation. For England, Northern Ireland and Scotland, between 11 and 14 per cent of looked-after children are in residential accommodation.

The remaining children have either been placed for adoption (5 per cent across the UK), and are living with their prospective adoptive family prior to the adoption becoming official, or else they are living independently or in other placements (5 per cent across the UK).

At 31 March 2002, there were 59,700 children who were looked after by English local authorities, compared to over 92,000 in 1981. (Following the Children Act 1989, implemented in 1991, numbers dropped but then climbed again to the 1991 level.) Of these, 39,200 were in foster care and 3,600 were living with prospective adoptive parents. Another 6,700 (11 per cent) were living at home with parents under the terms of a care order (Department of Health, 2003b). In Scotland, at 31 March 2001, 27 per cent of the looked-after children and young people were in foster care but a much larger number than in England and Wales were under compulsory supervision requirements but living at home (Scottish Executive, 2002). In Wales 75 per cent of children and young people were fostered (2,691 of 3,289) (Welsh Assembly, 2001). In Northern Ireland the rate of fostered children and young people is 63 per cent of the total of 2,414 (Department of Health, Social Services and Public Safety, 2001).

Over the last two decades, children have been remaining in care or accommodation for longer periods. Although a similar proportion as in the 1980s (80 per cent) leave care or accommodation within two years, they tend now to stay for longer within this two-year period. Ten thousand or so children have been looked after in foster care for more than one year (Department of Health, 2000). Rowe and colleagues (1989) and Stone (1995) painted a very different picture of placement length from that in the more recent study by Sinclair and others (2000). A decade or so ago somewhere between half and two-thirds of children, especially younger ones, were returning to live with their families within weeks or at most months. Sinclair and others (2000) found that 30 per cent of those approved as short-term and intermediate carers had children with them for more than 12 months; a further 23 per cent of children in this study were what local authorities described as in 'long-term' foster care.

Detailed information about the length of time spent in care and the number of placements experienced is available only for children looked after in England. Of these children, a quarter had been in the same placement for a year or less, but a further quarter had been in placements of longer than five years. Of children ceasing to be looked after during the year to 31 March 2001, a third had been cared for in a single placement. However, over 43 per cent had experienced 2-4 placements, 15 per cent 5-9 placements and 7 per cent 10 or more placements in the course of their care history. In the year ending March 2002, around 3,400 children were adopted from care in England, and it is estimated that there are around 5,000 more children awaiting adoption placements (Department of Health, 2003b).

The kind of children and young people in care today who are looked after by foster carers – or, for that matter, are available for adoption – has changed significantly over the years, as residential placements have decreased. Children and young people come into public care for a variety of reasons, and may have emotional difficulties and a spectrum of challenging behaviours. Their histories are complex and they are likely to have come from the most disadvantaged families in the country. Children in care are more likely to come from single-parent homes, fractured families, or be black or of mixed race, come from families on income support and where there is an experience of mental illness, and are more likely to be boys, or part of a large group of brothers and sisters.

Most children in care will have suffered one or more forms of abuse, and increasing numbers are the children of drug users and may themselves be born addicted. Infants may be looked after because they have older brothers or sisters in care who have been abused. Some will have learning difficulties or be physically disabled and others will have been excluded from school. Many children will have a cocktail of all of these factors to contend with in their early lives. The factor that they all share is that they have experienced early adversity and may display a range of behaviours that do not make it easy for them to fit into a family. To a greater or lesser extent they all present parenting challenges to their carers. In 2000/01, 43 per cent of children began to be looked after because of abuse and neglect (Department of Health, 2002).

Sinclair and colleagues have summed up the ways in which some children will express themselves:

> They might steal, lie, break things, have tantrums, refuse to eat, smear walls, wet their beds, refuse to bath, continually defy their carers, set light to their bedding, take overdoses, make sexual advances to other children, expose themselves in public, make false allegations, attack others, truant, take drugs or get into trouble with the police. (Sinclair et al, 2000, p4)

Foster care cannot be seen in isolation from other services. The Convention of Scottish Local Authorities has stated that foster care 'should be seen as part of the range of services offered to support families to care for their own children' (Convention of Scottish Local Authorities, 2000). The Welsh Assembly reiterated this view when it stated that 'foster care may also be provided alongside other services, for example family support, day care and residential services, including those provided by education and health, to implement children's care plans' (Welsh Assembly, 2002).

However, what Rowe and colleagues wrote nearly 15 years ago still holds true:

> The day to day, bread and butter work of fostering is still the placement of younger children needing care for a brief period during a family crisis or to give relief to hard-pressed parents. (Rowe et al, 1989, p79)

The roles and tasks of foster carers

As the characteristics of children for whom foster care is sought have changed, so have the tasks of foster carers, and fostering brings greater challenges than in the past. There is no comprehensive legal definition of short-term and intermediate foster care, so the tasks which foster carers perform define the nature of contemporary, time-limited foster care practice (these are listed by Sellick, 1992, Appendix A; and 1996, pp162–163).

Foster care tasks include:

- receiving children at short notice during family crises
- working inclusively with parents and with social workers and other professional staff
- providing high standards of direct care
- supporting parents and young people leaving care or accommodation.

Independent fostering agencies

The rapid expansion of independent fostering agencies during the 1990s has continued into the new century so that there are estimated to be as many of these organisations as there are local authority fostering agencies in England (Sellick, 2002). Once the preserve of the public and to some extent the voluntary childcare sector, fostering and foster carers are now a part of a mixed economy of provision. The early independent fostering agencies were established in Kent and grew from that local authority's specialist teenage scheme (Hazel and Fenyo, 1993). The sector expanded in an earlier political era where the development of non-public welfare services was encouraged, and statutory inspection and regulation were discouraged.

As local authorities continue to struggle to recruit and retain foster carers, the use of the independent sector, as well as kinship care, has been increased to fill this placement void. All fostering agencies across the public, independent and private sectors are now required to be registered, and to be inspected by the National Care Standards Commission which came into being on 1 April 2002.

The independent agencies are generally characterised by the extensive and high-quality services they provide to both their foster carers and the children placed. The authors of an evaluation study of one large agency and a subsequent national survey of 55 independent fostering agencies across mainland Britain commented on the range of support services to foster carers, including round-the-clock access to social workers and regular short-break care as well as the additional health, therapeutic and educational services provided to the children and young people (Sellick, 1999a; 2002; Sellick and Connolly, 2002).

Although there are currently no outcome studies which allow us to judge whether the care provided by independent fostering agencies is more successful than that provided by local authorities, foster carers and local authority social workers employed by them report very favourably on their practice. For many years foster carers have reported feeling valued and well supported, and social workers have spoken highly of the range and availability of child-focused services (Bebbington and Miles, 1990; Sellick, 1992; 1999a). A recent study confirms that while local authority foster carers often reported that they did not feel valued by social workers or listened to by their agency staff their peers in the independent agencies were by contrast satisfied in relation to these areas of support from their agencies (Kirton et al, forthcoming).

Recent research has challenged conventional wisdom that the independent fostering agencies are 'private enterprises which poach local authority foster carers who then provide children and young people with unplanned placements where none are available locally' (Sellick and Connolly, 2002, p117). This national survey found that the majority of these agencies were in the voluntary and charitable sectors, that only 33 per cent of foster carers were directly recruited to them from local authorities, and that almost one third of the children and young people had been placed on a planned basis for a long-term placement, often with their siblings or in order to be raised by carers of the same ethnicity.

The Department of Health is currently exploring options for delivering foster care and related services to children and young people through the Choice Protects programme. The Social Care Institute for Excellence (SCIE) has commissioned studies to inform the review. Although at the time of writing this book (summer 2003) nothing has been formally decided, it is clear that this mixed economy of foster care is likely to endure and be underpinned by government policy. In January 2003, the Department of Health announced a new investment of £113 million over three years.

Researching the outcomes of temporary foster care

It is important to remember that an attempt is being made here to apply academic rigour to a generally untidy subject:

> The notion of outcomes when human beings are involved is never a 'neat package' but one with pluses and minuses. Total success or total failure can only be found with a few cases at the extremes. For the rest it is mainly a picture of 'benefits and losses' knowing that there are still many gaps in our knowledge about the answers to some important questions. (Triseliotis et al, 1995, p15)

Most research studies and the published accounts of practice before the mid-1980s were about long-term foster care. While there have been several studies since then about temporary foster care, most have been small-scale and mainly descriptive rather than evaluative. When viewed together, these studies tell us a good deal about the changing nature of the short-term and intermediate or temporary fostering task, the skills and qualities required of competent foster carers and, in turn, what they value or seek from social workers and fostering agencies in the statutory, voluntary and independent childcare sectors. Some studies also give indications of how foster carers and birth parents can be helped by social workers to work co-operatively to get children safely back home.

Outcome measures in short-term and intermediate foster care

There are numerous interacting variables that may have an impact on the success or otherwise of short-term and intermediate foster placement. These include the characteristics of:

- the children being placed
- parenting and any maltreatment to which the children have been exposed
- the birth parents

- the social work service with parents, children and carers before, during and after placement
- the foster carers.

The main outcome measure used is whether or not the placement broke down or lasted as long as was needed, but a range of outcome measures can be used in more qualitative studies. It is difficult to link reliably long-term client outcomes to short-term and intermediate interventions, and the following are examples of indicators of success used by researchers.

What did it mean for the child?
- Did the placement last as long as needed?
- Was the child, according to his or her understanding, enabled to participate in decisions affecting the placement?
- Was 'comfortable contact' achieved for the child with members of the birth family and with friends from school and home community?
- Did the child's well-being improve as a result of the placement?
- Was the child able to continue with his or her preferred leisure activities?
- Were the child's health and educational needs met as well as or more successfully in the foster placement than before?
- Was the child's identity, including racial, cultural and religious identity, respected?
- Was the child enabled to return home or to move to a new family with the minimum of stress and disruption?
- Was the child generally satisfied with the placement?

What did it mean for the wider birth family?
- Did the parent play a full part in decisions about the options for the child, including the foster placement?
- Did the parent feel fully involved in the day-to-day decisions affecting their child?
- Did the parent feel confident that the child was safe and well cared-for physically and emotionally?
- Was the parent encouraged and supported both by the foster carers and social worker to maintain comfortable contact with their child?
- Did the parent retain their attachment to the child, and was their relationship with the child improved?

- Whatever the child's care status, did the parent retain a sense of parental authority and responsibility?
- Did the parent make use of the temporary absence of the child to resolve any difficulties?
- Was the well-being of the parent at least no worse (and preferably better) following the foster placement?
- Were the parenting skills of the primary carers and their self-confidence as parents at least no worse (and preferably better) at the end of the placement?
- Was the parent able to assimilate the child back into the family with minimal stress to all family members?
- Was the parent satisfied with the placement?

What did it mean for the foster carers?
- Was the child's placement a successful experience for the foster carers in terms of providing the rewards that they hoped to get out of fostering?
- Did the foster carers' own children enjoy and feel a part of the fostering experience?
- Did the placement last for the length of time originally planned?
- Did the foster carers believe themselves to be fully involved in the day-to-day decisions affecting the child in placement?
- Were the foster carers sensitively and effectively supported by the social worker and the fostering agency?
- Were the foster carers able to use their knowledge, skills and experience to the benefit of the child?
- Overall, did the placement add to the foster carers' skills and confidence?
- Was the well-being of the foster carers and their children at least no less (and preferably greater) as a result of their foster caring?
- Are the foster carers able to transfer learning from this and previous placements to future ones?

What did it mean for the agency?
- As a result of the placement, did the foster carers agree to continue to foster or make an informed choice to stop fostering?
- Did the placement last as long as planned, thus avoiding the need for a further placement to be found?
- Did the placement last longer than planned and, if so, was this because of lack

of time, skill or commitment on the part of carers or social worker to work towards the agreed aims?
- Were all the relevant statutory regulations and departmental procedures followed during the course of the placement?
- Were effective collaborative working practices maintained for the benefit of the child and family by both the social worker and other professional staff involved?

Research evidence for 'what works' in short-term and intermediate foster care

Four questions can be used to consider the evidence of 'what works' in temporary fostering.

- What do we know about the effectiveness of short-term and intermediate care for children generally, and for particular groups of children including children from black and minority ethnic backgrounds, disabled children, adolescents and children who have been abused?
- How successful is short-term and intermediate foster care as a method of family support?
- How can foster care contribute to the successful return of children to their birth families, or a realisation of other permanent plans?
- What do we know about effectiveness in the recruitment and retention of short-term and intermediate foster carers who meet the needs of children?

Research findings can be used to draw some general conclusions about what models of practice appear most likely to lead to successful outcomes.

Effectiveness of short-term and intermediate care

Although the study by Jane Rowe and colleagues (1989) took place before the Children Act, which became law that year, it remains the major research work into short-term and intermediate foster care. Rowe and colleagues studied 3,796 foster placements over a period of 24 months (Table 1). 'Successful' placements were defined as those in which the aims were described by social workers as being achieved fully or in most respects.

Because so few evaluative studies of short-term and intermediate foster care have been undertaken, there is very little British research that relates outcomes for children, or achievement of service aims, with the different variables. Berridge and

Table 1 **Types and frequencies of short-term and intermediate fostering, and their success rates**

Category placement	Number	%	% successful
Temporary care	1,471	46	88
Emergency/roof over head	446	14	83
Preparation for long-term placement	440	14	79
Assessment	402	13	57
Treatment	299	9	46
Bridge to independence	140	4	53
Total	**3,198**	**100**	

Adapted from Rowe et al (1989)

Note: 15 per cent of this cohort (598 placements) were long-term, and so are excluded from this table

Cleaver's (1987) study associated success in short-term and intermediate placements with factors such as more rigorous selection procedures for foster carers, sensitively managed matching and introductions, regular contact between children and their families, more frequent visits by link social workers to foster carers and greater efforts by social workers in working with the child's family.

Race and ethnicity

In her review of the literature on black children in local authority care, Ravinder Barn (1990) highlighted the dated and inadequate nature of the available information on this topic, and the degree to which black children's concerns have been overlooked. Her study of the care careers of children in one local authority (Barn, 1993a) found that black and white children generally take different paths. Black children were more likely to be placed with foster carers, had more regular parental contact and most entered the care system with the consent of their parents rather than under compulsion. More recent research has identified ethnicity and culture as important variables, but numbers in cohort studies are usually still small.

Bebbington and Miles (1989) found that children of mixed parentage were over-represented in their large cohort of children who entered local authority care and accommodation. Chand and others (2003), using the latest available population and Department of Health statistics on children who are looked after, concluded that children with two African-Caribbean parents, two African parents or one white and one black parent were over-represented, but that Bangladeshi, Indian and East Asian children were under-represented among those children who are looked after.

Rowe and colleagues (1989) found that although children of African-Caribbean origin were disproportionately represented in admissions to care, this was mainly accounted for by the large number of young black children being admitted for temporary voluntary care (in pre-Children-Act terms) during family emergencies. They stayed only a short time and went home again.

In the study of 944 foster carers by Sinclair and colleagues (2000), the response rate from the minority ethnic carers was lower than that of the white carers. The largest group of minority ethnic respondents (3.7 per cent) was African-Caribbean; 1.0 per cent were Asian; 0.8 per cent of mixed parentage; 0.8 per cent Indian; 0.5 per cent Bangladeshi; and 0.2 per cent Pakistani. Of the 596 foster children on whom data were obtained, 22 per cent were of minority ethnic origin, the largest proportion (7.2 per cent) being of mixed parentage.

Although increasing numbers of African-Caribbean carers are now being attracted and approved for fostering, some minority ethnic groups are still under-represented among foster carers. While there is more success in placing African-Caribbean children with carers of the same background, this is not always the case with Asian children or with children of mixed parentage (Caesar et al, 1994). However, some targeted initiatives have led to significant gains in the recruitment and retention of Asian foster carers (Almas, 1991).

Evaluative studies of foster care for black and Asian children tend to be restricted to studies of the success in recruiting families from different ethnic groups. Measures of success in terms of outcomes for children, such as improved well-being or social or cultural identity, are little studied. Caesar and colleagues (1994) touch on these, but numbers of cases studied are very small.

Qualitative researchers have identified factors that may lead to stability and security for black children. Among these are regular contact with birth families and/or brothers and sisters placed elsewhere, and understanding and empathy by the foster carers (Barn, 1993a; Barn et al, 1997; Thoburn et al, 2000). However, there is little evidence from research that can show us the risk and protective factors in placements of short or intermediate length and how these are experienced by children from different ethnic backgrounds.

Barn (2001), however, finds that where local authorities have invested adequate resources in the areas identified as important within the Children Act – race, culture, religion and language – certain minority-group children stand a good chance of being placed in foster family settings, and, more specifically, in families which reflect their own cultural background (Barn, 1993a; Barn et al, 1997). She writes:

> Mixed-parentage children present a particular dilemma for social services. The vast majority of mixed-parentage children who enter the care system come from a single-parent family. In such cases, the single parent tends to be the white birth mother and the absent father African Caribbean. The mixed-parentage child may have little or no contact with their black relatives. (Barn, 2001, p23)

Barn and colleagues (1997) found that children of mixed parentage were equally likely to be placed with a black or a white family. This led social workers to ask whether such a child was in a transracial placement. Barn (2001), summarising this work, says that:

> The categorisation on the basis of 'race' and ethnicity, and the practices of 'same race' and transracial placements required more complex thinking in the situation of children whose ethnic background was 'mixed', and thus challenged the boundaries of racialised identities. Barn et al (1997) noted that placement decisions with regard to mixed-parentage children were, at times, being made within simplistic notions of 'race' and colour. For example, factors such as skin shade were taken as an indicator of where the child should be placed rather than the long-term needs of the child within a holistic and ecological framework. (Barn, 2001, p24)

Disabled children

There is only limited research on what works for children with physical and learning disabilities who are fostered. It falls into two broad categories, concerning: short-term and intermediate, shared short-break care (for example, by Stalker, 1990; Beresford et al, 1996; Beresford, 2002) and permanent family placements for severely disabled young people (for example, Ames, 1993).

The following factors have been associated with successful short-break care (Oswin, 1984; Bayley, 1987; Robinson, 1987; and Stalker, 1990):

- local placements which avoid the need to change schools
- good-quality care which is age-appropriate
- available placements on demand when parents need a break
- placements which remain short term
- recognition of the child's individual personality in designing the placement package which is in turn a part of an integrated programme of family support
- carefully planned care, in terms of quantity, purpose and duration.

A number of factors have emerged from the research that are common to both ends of the placement continuum. Success appears to be associated with good preparation and matching of carers, and with social work support of the foster carers including the practical recognition of the impact on the birth children of the foster carers (Argent, 1998).

CASE STUDY 1

Previous experience useful: caring and disability

Barnardo's Breakaway service in Dudley began in 1985 when a local paediatrician asked for help in finding permanent family placements for children who had been in a long-stay hospital. Local people with knowledge of the hospital and people with understanding of disability came forward in the first tranche of carers. The service now finds that carers with previous experience of disability are particularly well placed to understand and cope with the complex care needs of severely disabled children. Among their current carers are people who have disabled family members, and a former nurse who had worked with children with severe learning disabilities. They have a good understanding of the children's complex care needs and the project has continued to attract carers with a special and prior understanding of the needs of disabled children.

Adolescents and young offenders

Although most adolescents are not in specialist schemes, despite the large numbers of adolescents in care, much research and practice attention has been paid to the foster placement of teenage children in both the UK (Shaw and Hipgrave, 1983;

Hazel, 1990; Lowe, 1990; Hazel and Fenyo, 1993; Walker et al, 2002) and in North America (Hill et al, 1993 and Nutter et al, 1993b). A survey of local authority fostering arrangements (Waterhouse, 1997) confirmed an earlier survey carried out for the National Foster Care Association (Lowe, 1990) in finding that most local authorities do have specialist fostering schemes for adolescents. Similarly, the social work staffing of these schemes is generous in relation to the numbers of children involved when these are compared with the far greater numbers of younger children in mainstream foster care.

Developments in the use of foster care as an alternative to custody or secure accommodation have been scrutinised in recent research. For example, Sellick and Connolly (2002), in their national survey, found that just over half of all independent fostering agencies offered remand placements to local authorities. A Scottish study of specialist family placements for young people presenting a risk to themselves or to others found that well-supported foster carers can help to 'turn their lives around in a major way' (Walker et al, 2002, p223).

Remand fostering is a growing area of practice. Utting and Vennard (2000) included this kind of fostering in their review of what works with young offenders in the community. Although the authors are generally cautious about the transferability of evidence from the USA, they cite the success of a structured remand fostering programme in that country which recruits and trains specialist foster carers to supervise, manage and reward behaviour and structure leisure time and contact with young people of the same age and background. The evaluation (Chamberlain 1990, cited by Utting and Vennard 2000) indicates lower arrest rates for young people fostered in this way than for those who were given some kind of group care, and lower rates of imprisonment for those fostered than those given other types of community placement.

Utting and Vennard (2000) report that, in Britain, schemes such as the Wessex (Hampshire) Community Remand Project, a partnership between NCH and Wessex (Hampshire) Youth Offending Team, are also managing to recruit and retain foster carers. Evidence, they say, is beginning to emerge that the schemes have a good record in reducing offending for the duration of the placement, even for serious and repeat offenders. The authors conclude that remand fostering schemes build on the evidence that parents and 'significant' adults who use positive reinforcement and consistent sanctions can reduce anti-social behaviour in children and young people.

Sexual abuse and fostering

Many agencies share concerns about practice when placing children who have been sexually abused. One study interviewed 66 foster and adoptive families and made wide-ranging recommendations for practice in this area with children, their carers and their birth children (Macaskill, 1991). These related to the preparation and training of carers, helping children to talk about their abuse, and dealing with allegations against carers. Major concerns are expressed about two important matters: the risk of recruiting carers who are paedophiles; and exposing carers and their families to the stresses which result from caring for a child who behaves in a sexualised way, or who wrongly accuses carers of sexual or physical abuse of children.

There is little direction in the literature in terms of work on the first concern. Some agencies, however, are acknowledging that media advertising may attract child abusers and are devising practice guidelines (see for example, Irving and Joss, 1995; Irving, 1996). Police checks as a way of ensuring that those who work with children do not have relevant criminal convictions have been in use for many years. In 1997 the discretion was removed from local authorities to allow people with a Schedule 1 offence to act as foster carers following the conviction in Wales of Roger Saint, a foster carer and adoptive parent, for numerous sexual offences against children in his care. (There has also been an easing of the ban in relation to those related to children where the offence was many years ago, and would not now be considered relevant.) Preventive measures like these will go some way towards disqualifying those who have a criminal conviction, but concern must continue about those who have not.

There is a growing literature base on both the prevention of child sexual abuse by foster carers and the manner in which allegations are handled. Practice guidance is produced by many fostering agencies and by the Fostering Network (National Foster Care Association, 1993a). An early example of a practice guide is Davis and colleagues' (1987) for the Barnardo's North East Division. An indication of international concern is found in the number of presentations on both alleged and actual abuse by carers at the Ninth International Conference of the International Foster Care Organisation from countries such as Norway and Canada (International Foster Care Organisation, 1995). In 2000, BAAF Adoption and Fostering radically revised Form F, the carer assessment form widely used for adopters and foster carers, to ensure that evidence was provided of checks with applicants' employers, previous partners and adult children living elsewhere.

The National Foster Care Association (NFCA) also took part in an international survey of foster carers about abuse allegations in the USA, Canada and Europe (Verity and Nixon, 1995; 1996). Foster carers reported that they considered themselves to have been poorly informed, that investigations took a long time to complete, and that the outcome was often unspecified. In a study into how one large local authority investigated allegations of all abuse against its approved foster carers (Nixon, 1997) a difference emerged between the attitudes and approaches of link social workers and children's social workers in relation to the thresholds of alleged abuse by carers. Link workers were more inclined to maintain a higher threshold even when this appears to be at odds with their agency's guidelines on child protection.

Short-term and intermediate foster care as a method of family support
The problems of defining and measuring success were discussed in Chapter 1. Some studies (for example, Berridge and Cleaver, 1987) use breakdown rates as a measure of success or failure, whereas others look at whether the placement has lasted as long as planned, or too long (for example, Rowe et al, 1989). Table 2 below (in Chapter 3 page 58) includes a range of potential outcome measures which may be used in surveys and qualitative research. Fifteen per cent of the sample of children in short-term and intermediate foster care in Stone's (1995) study were long-stayers in what was intended to be a short placement; another 12 per cent moved between temporary placements and an overlapping 13 per cent moved to a short-term and intermediate placement from another placement in care.

Defining helpfulness is more straightforward, especially in consumer studies. The parents interviewed in the study by Aldgate and Bradley (1999) remarked on the friendliness and supportiveness of foster carers, their generosity and their non-judgemental approach. These qualities were viewed as contributing to the restoration of parents' self-esteem and confidence. Two carers in Sellick's study (1992) saw themselves as shared carers with families (even though they were not part of a formal short-break care scheme within their agency) and related this aspect of their work to supporting families. Their views are supported by research in Sweden where foster carers play a major role as providers of support to families in need and this has led to a significant decrease in the use of compulsory care measures (Baddredine and Idstrom, 1995).

The majority of the short-break carers in the study by Aldgate and Bradley (1999) reported that working with parents was a significant part of their work that they found both rewarding and demanding. The difficulties they faced included the level of dependency that could develop, the expression of hostility and ambivalence towards themselves and their own families and the ways in which parents behaved towards the children.

Going home or moving on: temporary care and permanency

Few British research studies explicitly describe the elements of foster care practice that are specifically aimed at moving children back home or to new families, and even fewer attempt to evaluate this practice. Most of the outcome studies on this topic are North American, largely because, in North America, the major 'permanence' option has long been recognised as the return home of children from foster care. Therefore, research studies on the introduction of permanence policies in the USA include data on variables associated with children returning home. Stein and colleagues (1978), Lahti (1982), Fein and colleagues (1983), and Jones (1985) all involve fairly high numbers, which allow for some analysis of the variables which appear to be associated with whether the children returned home, remained in foster care or moved to a new family. Some, most notably Stein and colleagues (1978), Jones (1985) and Fein and colleagues (1983), and more recently Pine and colleagues (2002), describe in detail the practice which appears to be associated with successful return home.

Maluccio and colleagues (1986) describe their work in a practice text more widely available in the UK, *Permanency planning for children: concepts and methods*. This approach to practice, which comes under the broad heading of an 'ecological model', emphasises the competence rather than the problems of families and makes extensive use of written agreements. Jones' (1985) research found that a 'preventive maintenance' approach to family social work was associated with both keeping children out of placement and enabling a quicker return home for those who did have to be placed away from their families.

The work of Stein and colleagues (1978) is described in more detail in the first book of this 'What works?' series (Macdonald and Roberts, 1995). It is an example of one of the few randomised controlled trials in child and family social work research. While Jones compared different methods, the research by Stein and colleagues was an evaluation of the Alameda Project that used behavioural methods and a task-centred approach in a concerted attempt to reduce the length of time which children spent in unplanned foster care. There are similarities between this model and that described by Maluccio and colleagues in that both emphasise the use of agreements. However, the ecological approach, and the practice concluded by Jones to be more effective, places more emphasis on the empowerment of parents and less on a time-limited service.

All studies conclude that practice that succeeds in keeping parents and children in comfortable contact with each other is associated with the return home of the child. Indeed, despite the detailed description of practice in the studies by Jones and by Stein and colleagues, it is still not clear whether it is the practice method used or the maintenance of contact between parents and children which is the key variable, since both are integral to the package of helping methods evaluated.

Contact stands out from a range of USA and UK research as the key variable independently associated with return home. Jenkins and Norman (1972) used the term 'filial deprivation' to describe the state of mind of the parents of children in foster care they interviewed as part of a major American study which was later written up by Fanshel and Shinn (1978). These two studies were influential in condemning the 'let's wait and see if they are really interested' approach to parental visiting which was widespread at the time.

Contact as a possible influence on the return home of children from care has been studied more widely in the UK than have practice methods. Thoburn (1980) concluded from a small qualitative study that some families remained in contact with their children despite the poor service they received. The determination of parents and children to stay in touch with each other led to return home. Thorpe (1980) and Aldgate (1980), in two early UK studies, did find associations between the service provided to parents (specifically the emotional and practical support which social workers provided to help them to visit their children), and the maintenance of contact.

The prospective longitudinal study of Millham and colleagues (1986) gives detailed accounts of how foster carers and social workers either facilitated contact or allowed it to fade away. Cleaver (2000) provided a detailed account of services which contributed to appropriate contact with birth relatives following the Children Act 1989 and notes much improvement in the frequency of contact since the earlier studies.

Bullock and others (1993) combined the group of 450 children in the study by Millham and colleagues (1986) with 320 children studied by Farmer and Parker (1991) and 161 studied by Packman (1986). They concluded that around 90 per cent of children who started to be looked after by a local authority would return home, either to their parents' care or to the home environment as young adults, although some came back into care for shorter or longer times (Sinclair et al, 2000; Harwin and Owen, 2003). They were able with these larger numbers to list the variables associated with children returning home quickly or after longer intervals, and with them remaining safely at home after return. Qualitative interviews add detail about practice to the statistical data, and Farmer and Parker contributed information about practice from a scrutiny of the files. A Northern Ireland study by Pinkerton (1994) also describes practice associated with children who return home 'on trial'. Packman and Hall (1998), who scrutinised policy and social work practice following the Children Act 1989 when children are accommodated, also provide guidance on what children and parents found helpful.

The kind of practice reported in these studies to be most likely to get children back home safely is encouragingly similar.

- Good practice starts even before the child leaves home, with a carefully negotiated agreement and choice of placement informed by the wishes of child and parents. The implication of this is clear – avoid, if at all possible, the emergency admissions that preclude such planning.
- The existence of close working relationships between the social worker for the children, the carer's link worker, the foster carers and the parents and older children is the central feature of practice which succeeds in reuniting families.
- Contracts or agreements are considered by all researchers to be vital ingredients of this model of practice and have been incorporated into the Regulations and Guidance accompanying the Children Act. The review process is pivotal, but it has to be a process and not simply an event. In other words, the casework practice and negotiations which go on before, during and after each review are centrally important if the agreement is to lead to actions being taken which will result in the necessary change in the behaviour of the children or parents, or in their practical circumstances.
- Farmer and Parker (1991) also concluded that the chances of successful return home were increased if social workers maintained a clear sense of purpose, together with a readiness to use their authority when appropriate.

In a chapter summarising the research on achieving permanence for children returning home, Thoburn (1994a) lists the following characteristics which have been associated by more than one researcher with successful return:

- the child being under the age of 2 when returned home
- the parents having regular contact with the child while he or she was away;
- the parents attending reviews when the child was away
- the parents being willing to talk to each other and the social worker about the problems they may encounter when the child returns home
- no serious new problems in relation to childcare emerging while the child was away from home or after return
- no younger step- or half-sibling at home when the child returned
- the child continuing to have a role in the family throughout the stay away, for example, by keeping toys or clothes at home, and having his or her bedroom or at least some personal space.

All the researchers stress that variables interact in unpredictable ways and that check-lists should not be rigidly applied. All emphasise, in particular, that different issues have to be taken into account with children of different ages, and in the light of any maltreatment that they have experienced and may be vulnerable to on return home.

Two qualitative studies by social workers at Barnardo's Colchester New Families project are important sources of information about practice. Jackie Trent's (1989) study evaluated the application of the methods and skills normally used to place children with new families to getting some of those referred for permanent family placement safely back with their birth parents or relatives. Jane Westacott's (1988) study describes and evaluates the work of 'bridge' families. While most of the children are 'bridged' into placements with new families, an important aspect of the practice of these foster carers involves working in partnership with social workers and parents to get children safely home. Although several of the research studies on permanent family placement have something to say about the role of temporary carers in preparing children and new parents for the move, the study by Westacott is one of the few which specifically focuses on the 'bridging' role of foster carers.

Finding them, keeping them: recruitment and retention of foster carers

Research carried out since the late 1990s has increased knowledge about what is needed to find and keep supplementary foster carers. This section looks at research findings on what works in recruitment, assessment, training and support.

Recruitment

The first edition of this book (Sellick and Thoburn, 1996) highlighted three key recruitment messages drawn from existing research studies.

- Success in recruiting an adequate number of high-quality foster carers is associated with targeted schemes.
- Fostering agencies have to respond in an efficient and businesslike way to sustain the interest of potential foster carers.
- The initial recruitment process is associated with retention.

More recent studies have continued to review effectiveness from the perspective of foster carers and have added much to what we know in this area.

According to John Triseliotis and colleagues (2000) the low profile of fostering within many Scottish local authorities had an adverse effect on policy development and resourcing in Scotland. One in four agencies, including those serving the more highly populated areas, were experiencing serious shortages of carers. Recruitment was largely one-off and unsystematic with no long-term direction or strategy. The most successful methods, however, were local. Word of mouth was confirmed as the most effective method of attracting foster carers (53 per cent), while 22 per cent of existing carers were alerted to fostering by reading articles in the local press. This research finding does not sit well with the £2 million UK government-funded foster care recruitment campaign of 2001. The results were officially described as 'disappointing' (National Foster Care Association, 2001). From a research perspective, this is unsurprising, and managers of fostering agencies would do well to note that as many as 75 per cent of carers can be recruited cheaply and effectively through word of mouth and local press activities.

Sinclair and colleagues (2000) found that as many as 20 per cent of registered foster carers across seven local authorities were not fostering at the time of their study. Sellick and Connolly (2002) found evidence of these dormant foster carers being recruited by independent agencies. Foster carers in the Scottish study felt that if they played a central role in recruitment, they could address more effectively the commonly held public fears and stereotypes concerning fostering and social work. This approach may make recruitment more successful, especially in urban areas, where the need is highest but recruitment is lowest.

CASE STUDY 2

Recruiting foster carers across a group of local authorities

Following a period of concern about the quality of foster placements offered by the voluntary and private sector, the East Midlands Fostering Consortium commissioned Barnardo's to develop criteria for approval, and draw up a list of approved placement agencies. Eventually, a service was developed to work across several authorities. The service aims to provide long-term and permanent placements for children who have been hard to place: brothers and sisters; children from black and minority ethnic backgrounds; older children, particularly boys aged between 9 and 13 – some who have been sexually abused and others who have sexually problematic behaviour towards other children.

An initial plan for recruitment was to pool funds and advertise for each authority in turn. The first campaign was funded by one member of the consortium and focused on recruiting carers for that authority. However, this approach would have meant a long wait for some members, and subsequent recruitment was planned for a 40–50-mile radius of the service. This takes in all but one of the authorities, and placements will generally be offered within the authority where the carer lives but very urgent needs across the consortium will have priority, for example to achieve stability for a child where the transfer to secondary school is looming.

Although in its infancy, the reasonably swift establishment of the service is credited in part to the lack of start-up costs for the member authorities, as these were borne by Barnardo's. The East Midlands Fostering Consortium identifies the following factors enabling its overall success:

- good continuity of membership, stable for the first two to three years
- the support of the regional branch of the Association of Directors of Social Services which agreed priorities of improving practice, shaping future strategic approaches, monitoring the development of the independent sector, and advising on national initiatives
- membership at principal officer or equivalent status
- geographical similarities and strong regional identity
- single-issue focus on fostering which means that specialist fostering issues can be discussed without loss of interest
- coterminosity with the boundaries of the regional Social Services Inspectorate.

Assessment

Different theoretical frameworks have influenced the assessment of applications from potential foster carers. These range from the psychodynamic and the task-centred to the competence-based approaches, with a mixed methodology incorporating individual, couple and group components. One approach relies on a systemic family-therapy approach related to outcome research on what works and proposes a detailed six-session working model (McCracken and Reilly, 1998). Earlier research (for example, Triseliotis and colleagues 1995) described the interplay between the qualities and capacity of foster carers and the experiences and behaviour of children. The systemic family-therapy approach has been adapted to take full account of family functioning, including the position of the applicants' children, to supplement the traditional assessment features such as checks, references and medical examinations.

Sir William Utting undertook an official review of the safeguards for children living away from home in the wake of successive abuse inquiries. His report, *People like us* (Utting, 1997) concluded that although care is taken in the selection of foster carers, the isolated nature of foster care has rendered children particularly vulnerable to abuse. The report recommended that a code of practice should be produced, taking account of current knowledge about sexual abusers and how they operate, and which pays particular regard to safeguarding children as far as possible. It also stressed that potential foster carers should understand the role that they are accepting, and should be required to demonstrate, as far as possible, the skills that they have for working with vulnerable children.

The code of practice on the recruitment, assessment, approval, training, management and support of foster carers was drawn up by a UK-wide foster care standards working party and endorsed by the Department of Health. It recommends using a competency approach to the assessment of children (National Foster Care Association, 1999). A task description and a list of 14 key competencies needed by carers gives clarity to applicants and assists them in considering how their life experiences can be used for the benefit of children. This gives the fostering agency considering the application a clearer picture of the skills of applicants of the training and support they will need to ensure a successful outcome for children. Various materials for the use of assessing social workers, applicants and panel members have been produced, providing practical tools for competency-based assessment, in accordance with the recommendations of the code of practice.

The competency framework for assessment provides the starting point for the annual reviews of foster carers, and should be linked to the training programmes developed for foster carers. It is also useful preparation for carers undertaking NVQs, or who are part of a skills payment scheme that is based on a competency model.

Nixon (1997; 2000) explored the support provided to foster carers who had experienced an allegation of abuse against themselves and/or a member of their immediate family. He recommended that, as early as the assessment stage, applicants should be made aware of the potential of such allegations. Although this may deter some applicants, others would see it as a good example of openness and honesty and as a first stage towards the later use of experienced foster carers in the training and support of other carers.

Training

Triseliotis and colleagues (2000) concluded from their research that foster carers who received a fee were more likely to support the idea of a salaried fostering service, to attend training and support groups, and to recognise that there were benefits for children in seeing their parents. They were also more satisfied with the operation of the fostering service. Preparation and training were well received, but, like carers in earlier studies, they wanted a more coherent and structured form of continuing training. The issue of dealing with difficult behaviour emerged from one study where foster carers commonly sought training on how to cope with anxious, depressed, aggressive or delinquent children and young people, or, as Sinclair and colleagues put it, 'training on issues which ordinary parents may not face' (Sinclair et al, 2000, p4).

In another study (Minnis et al, 1999), a randomised controlled trial was conducted to assess the impact of foster carer training on the attitudes of foster carers and on children's behaviour. An initial evaluation of the training programme of trained foster carers indicated success in that the content of the programme enabled them to understand and communicate more effectively with foster children and to participate in the process of joint training with social workers. Pithouse and colleagues (2002) found no evidence from their 'semi-experimental' investigation or a review of literature on training programmes for foster carers that they resulted in a more appropriate carer–child response. However, like Minnis and others (1999), they found that there was a high level of foster carer satisfaction with the programmes.

Foster carers in other studies have recommended that they become active participants in preparation training, to expose unrealistic expectations (Butler and Charles, 1999), and in continuing training, so that they may share their practice knowledge with others.

Support

Recent research has provided new information, usually from the perspective of foster carers, about the importance of support. Although Sinclair and colleagues (2000) were unable to show that support makes successful placements more likely, the combination of poor support, the complex needs of children and negative impacts upon foster carers does lead to a greater likelihood of placement breakdown, the departure of foster carers, or both. It is clear from the wider literature that support is linked to retention of foster carers. The role of the social worker – for the child, the family and the foster carers – remains pivotal. Good social workers 'talk and sort' as the researchers say (Sinclair et al, 2000, p4). Aldgate and Bradley defined this role in its relationship to carers and parents, where social workers 'engaged in the classic social work processes of assessment and intervention which are best described as social casework. This professional relationship was valued and used to good effect' (Aldgate and Bradley, 1999, p207).

The literature identifies three main sources of satisfaction or dissatisfaction with social workers (Sellick, 1999b; Fisher et al, 2000):

- their physical and emotional availability
- teamwork and respect
- help of a practical nature and with the individual child.

Fisher and colleagues (2000, p231) found that foster carers spoke positively of those social workers who:

- show an interest in how carers are managing
- are easy to contact and responsive when contacted
- do what they say they are going to do
- are prepared to listen and offer encouragement
- take account of the family's needs and circumstances
- keep them informed and include them in planning
- ensure that payments, complaints and so on are processed as soon as possible
- attend to the child's interests and needs and involve foster carers where appropriate.

Where face-to-face support from social workers was not possible, Fisher and colleagues (2000) found that foster carers were satisfied with regular telephone contact with them.

In addition to the importance of good support from social workers, the complementary need for mutual support between foster carers has been highlighted. Within the context of social work staff shortages and the priority given to child protection and other crisis work, Pithouse and colleagues (Pithouse et al, 1994; Pithouse and Parry, 1997) have emphasised the importance of foster carer support and self-help groups. Similarly, Nixon (2000) highlighted the importance of carer-to-carer support when allegations of malpractice are made.

Payment to foster carers has been widely researched in the UK (for example, Bebbington and Miles, 1990; Sellick, 1992). Pithouse and colleagues (1994, p45) found that systems of remuneration were both 'confused and confusing' and were linked to the status of foster carers as employees, volunteers or professionals. One small-scale study of 20 female foster carers concluded that 'the place of payment within foster care is likely to remain complex and controversial' (Kirton, 2001). Foster carers reported that payment did not motivate them to become foster carers, but that adequate and efficient payment systems kept them going when they felt dissatisfied by the children's behaviour or lack of progress.

'I think May and Bill needed the fostering allowance really. I suppose if it had been one child it would have been all right, but to look after three children and to pay rent, it helped. It helped us as well because we got clothes and goodness knows what else.'
FOSTERED YOUNG PERSON

'We started with the fostering allowance and they paid for the bunk beds. We were never told we could get a holiday allowance until the case was transferred back to the first local authority. We were never given the information we should have had. He was very destructive because he was very fidgety. She [the social worker] said: "He's a big lad – in teenage sizes when he was only ten. I'm going to have to make sure – to ask for more money, because he is so destructive with his clothes and sheets." And we got a lot more money then. I did find it helpful but I find it embarrassing. We didn't want a fostering allowance at first. By the time he was adopted we wanted to finish with them altogether. But by the time we adopted, we really needed it.'
FOSTER CARER WHO WENT ON TO ADOPT

Foster carers were found to perceive inadequate direct social work provision for children and foster carers as a key limitation of the overall social work service (Triseliotis et al, 2000). This is often contrasted with what is offered by some independent fostering agencies. Sellick's (1999a) evaluation of one large independent agency found that it offered additional services for children, including therapy, special education and contact and leisure facilities, and that local authority social workers valued these highly and commented frequently how well these services compared in terms of quality and availability with those in their own authorities.

Another important type of support is that which foster carers receive from their partners and relatives. Sinclair and colleagues (2000) found that, without such support, foster carers were more likely to give up fostering. Some local authorities have applied this research message by approving a relative, often a female foster carer's mother or sister, to provide them with a short-break care service.

Although the turnover of carers reported by Sinclair and others (2000) was low (about 10 per cent), the carers still experienced problems found in other research, including a lack of information about foster children, inefficiencies regarding payments and poor out-of-hours support. Turnover was low when there was good support by link workers, higher than average allowances or fees, and training and support from other carers. The study concluded that 'a combination of allowances, training, support from other carers and from family placement workers seems to provide the key to support' (Sinclair et al, 2000, p5).

Key messages about what works in short-term and intermediate foster care

- Success in short-term and intermediate placements comes from more rigorous selection procedures for foster carers, sensitively managed matching and introductions, regular contact between children and their families, more frequent visits by link social workers to foster carers, and greater efforts by social workers in working with the child's family.
- Black children and those of mixed parentage tend to take different paths in and out of placement from those taken by white children. Evaluative studies of foster care for black children tend to be restricted to studies of success in recruiting families from different ethnic groups. Child outcome measures of success are little studied.
- When short-term and intermediate care is used as a method of family support, foster carers can have an important role in working with parents and children in resolving difficulties.
- Contact is a key variable independently associated with successfully returning children from placement to their families.
- There is a lack of evaluative research into the effectiveness of strategies aimed at recruiting and retaining carers.
- There are specific required characteristics for foster carers, and recruitment messages that emphasise these characteristics may be more likely to attract people with the capabilities to become foster carers. This needs to be accompanied by clear information about the available package of training, support and remuneration.
- There are few studies of effectiveness of training carers. Research is needed which differentiates between types of training and evaluates the content, process and outcomes of the programmes.
- Support to carers is important in retaining carers and diminishing the number of placement breakdowns.

3 What works in long-term or permanent family placement?

There are two aspects of looking at practice in permanent family placement. The first is about decision-making. Where to place? What legal status? What sort of family? What sort of contact and with whom? The second aspect concerns social work practice, practical support and therapy to the child, birth relatives and new parents and members of their close family. What works in decision-making for adoptive and long-term foster placements will be considered first in this chapter, followed by what works in supporting long-term or permanent placements with foster and adoptive families (Thoburn, 2002).

Placement decisions and evidence about outcomes

Before exploring what works in decision-making, we consider how 'success' in permanent family placement might be defined. As with short-term placements, researchers have used a range of outcome measures. These are often dictated by the size of the sample and the research method. Surveys involving numbers large enough for statistical analysis often use placements lasting for a specific period of time as the only outcome measure. With qualitative research involving interviews and psychometric tests, the smaller numbers usually involved mean that placement breakdown rates for different groups, and analysis of variables associated with breakdown, have to be treated with caution. However, these studies can provide more detailed information on a range of measures of well-being and satisfaction and can make suggestions about the different sorts of practice that may be successful with different sorts of children and families. Thoburn (1990) found that for a small sample of placements assessed at least five years after placement, success rates varied depending on the outcome measure used (Table 2). This small sample could not provide reliable information on placement breakdown since it was weighted, as many interview samples are, towards those that lasted.

The decision about where to place a child is (or should be) closely bound up with the question of the likely outcome for the different placement options. The results of placing a child in a long-term or permanent family will depend very much on the characteristics of the child. Age at placement is a particularly important

Table 2 **Indicators of success in permanent family placement of 29 children (21 placed) five years after placement or referral**

	YES		NO	
	Number	%	Number	%
Did the placement last for 5 years?	19	90	2*	10
Was the child adopted?	16	76	5	24
Did the child have a 'sense of permanence'?	20	95	1	5
Did the parents have a 'sense of permanence'?	21	100	–	–
Did the child have a sense of personal identity?	16	76	5	24
Were there no serious concerns about the child's well-being?	14†	67	7	33
Did the child's well-being improve?	16	76	5	24
Was at least one parent well attached to the child?	18	85	3	15
Was the child well attached to at least one parent?	14	67	7	33
Had the child found a family for life?	19	90	2	10
Was the child satisfied with the placement?	17	81	4	19
Was the mother satisfied with the placement?	16	76	5	24
Was the father satisfied with the placement?	13	62	8	38
Were the natural children of the family satisfied? (12 placements only)	6	50	6	50
Was the placement successful? (overall rating of researcher)	18	86	3	14
What proportion of those referred were placed sucessfully overall?	18	62	11	38

*Two who left at 17 but were still in touch

†Includes three whose well-being was high before placement and remained so

Source: Thoburn (1990)

variable because it is a proxy for other variables. 'Proxy' here refers to the fact that when analysis is made in terms of the child's age, it is likely that other characteristics are being picked up that may have an impact on outcome. This is because children who are older also tend to have experienced more separations from people who were important to them, are more likely to have been maltreated, and are more likely to have emotional and behavioural problems. For example, a 6-week-old baby will probably have been placed before too much harm has been done. At the other extreme, teenagers are often on the move, even in 'ordinary' families, and most studies of the placement of teenagers show high rates of breakdown.

The larger the group studied, the more these individual differences can be allowed for when considering the relationship between any one variable and an outcome. Thus, from the larger-scale studies we have a better chance of determining whether, in most cases, a particular aspect of the service is associated with a successful outcome for a sub-group of children such as emotionally disturbed 12-year-old boys, or infants with Down's syndrome. (For a discussion on controlling for the impact of one variable on another, see the appendix by Sapsford in Fratter et al, 1991; Thoburn 1994a). Increasingly, researchers confront this problem from the start by evaluating placements for particular groups.

As mentioned in Chapter 2, official statistics for 2002 show that 5 per cent of the almost 78,000 children looked after by local authorities in the UK were living with adoptive parents prior to legal adoption by them. There are no national statistics on children placed with foster families with a view to adoption or the likelihood that this will be a permanent placement, possibly leading to an application for an adoption or residence order. Some indication of these proportions is provided by Sinclair and colleagues (2000), who found that nearly a quarter (23 per cent) of foster placements were described as long-term.

Some types of placement have received more attention than others, and some studies do not distinguish between the different sorts of children – for example, some North American studies of the placement of black children include children placed from overseas as well as children born in America. As will be discussed below, it has become increasingly clear that good outcomes are harder to obtain for some children than others. Thus, studies which give outcome information for undifferentiated groups of children are less useful than those which concentrate on particular groups of children, such as those who have learning disabilities, or are older at placement.

However, large numbers make it possible to use statistical techniques to differentiate between the outcomes for different groups.

Most studies examine both outcome and process, and reach conclusions about the sort of practice or the sorts of families that appear to be associated with better or worse outcomes for different groups of children. In contrast to the much less frequent study of temporary foster care, many researchers have evaluated permanent family placement work, and it is, therefore, more useful to concentrate on those which appear to have the most relevant evidence for British practice today. Some studies include only placements intended to be adoptive, while others include long-term or permanent foster placements.

The decision to place a child or young person with a new family is jointly made by some or all of the following: parents, young people, social workers, local authority solicitors, team managers, looked-after reviews, adoption and/or permanence panels and courts. There are descriptive accounts of these processes but no research that relates different processes to long-term outcomes for children. Four important recent UK studies that provide detailed descriptions of decision-making processes are:

- Lowe and others' (1999) survey of 115 adoption agencies placing children aged over 5 (including detailed postal survey responses from 226 adoptive families and some qualitative interviews)
- Neil's (2000b) survey of a 10 per cent sample of English children adopted under the age of 4 years
- Harwin and colleagues (2001) on care plans
- Lowe and Murch with others (2002) on the processes leading to some children being placed for long-term foster care and others for adoption.

Harwin and colleagues found that adoption plans were made for around a third of the children (all under 7, with an average age of less than 3 years). Attempts were made to implement these plans, but some had been changed to long-term foster care within a two-year period. Long-term foster care was the plan for just over a fifth of the children aged between 5 and 15, with an average age of 10 years. Just over one in ten were placed with relatives long-term.

Selwyn and colleagues (forthcoming) have carried out a three-year (2000–2003) study, one of 12 studies funded by the Department of Health to examine the costs and effectiveness of services to children in need, enabling a greater understanding of the reasons why adoption or long-term care is achieved more easily for some children than for others. They provide new evidence on the nature of costs at different points in the adoption process. The study uses a complete sample of 130 children approved for adoption when they were aged between 3 and 11 years. (Adoption studies rarely have complete samples and this will be one of the strengths of this study.) At the time of the follow-up in 2000/01, 80 of the children had been adopted, 34 were in other forms of permanent placements and 16 had experienced unstable care careers.

Long-term or permanent placement with foster carers

'We were supposed to be here for six months in the beginning and when the six months was up, I asked her [foster carer] whether we would be staying or going. I told her we were happy here. That was the only time I can remember talking about fostering. It wasn't discussed on a daily basis.'

FOSTERED YOUNG PERSON

'We didn't like it much when they came to see us at the foster home because it would mean that we had to come in from playing, and no one else was seeing social workers, so it used to be a bit of a pain. Sometimes I and my brother, we would just go, we just didn't want to see social workers. When they used to come we didn't do anything – we would just sit in the house and talk; it was quite boring really. We had to stay in for like an hour and talk about rubbish. We didn't have anything to say to them. We were really happy where we were. Now could we go out and play? That was it, really.'

FOSTERED YOUNG PERSON

There are two broad categories of permanent placement with non-relative foster carers. The most successful on a range of measures is the confirmation of an already existing 'temporary' foster placement as a permanent foster or adoptive placement. When such placements are included in a sample of 'permanent placements', as in the Lothian study (Borland et al, 1991) and several American studies (for example, Festinger, 1986; Barth and Berry, 1988), the breakdown rate is lower than when all the placements studied are with people not previously known to the children. This is explained by the fact that, if foster carers have become sufficiently attached to the child that they seek to be confirmed as permanent carers, the placement already starts off with a high likelihood of success. This is not to suggest that short-term placements should be left to drift on into long-term placements without proper assessment of whether this is the appropriate home for the child. Vernon and Fruin

(1985) and Millham and colleagues (1986) have suggested that short-term foster carers who really wish to be long-term carers consciously or unconsciously 'squeeze the birth parents out' and prevent restoration work from succeeding.

In a review of the literature, Schofield and colleagues (2000) found limited information about how children in long-term foster care fared, even though, as several studies of looked-after children make clear, this is by far the most common long-term option for children who cannot go safely home. Since the earlier foster care studies of the 1960s and 1970s reported high breakdown rates, long-term foster care has fallen into disrepute in the UK and North America, though not in most European countries. However, there have been several reports of considerable improvements in the success rates of 'ordinary' long-term placements. Rowe and colleagues (1989), Berridge and Cleaver (1987), Aldgate (1990) and Kelly (1995) all found that when age was held constant, breakdown rates were not dissimilar from those reported by other researchers for older children placed for adoption.

Surveys of adolescents with a range of problems – offending, homelessness and teenage pregnancy – have found that children who were once in foster care are greatly over-represented. However, this mainly reflects the fact that a large proportion of young people are already experiencing difficulties, often involving homelessness and criminal behaviour, at the point of entering care. No large-scale longitudinal study has yet been completed in the UK of a group of foster placements made with the intention that the children will remain in care until at least 16 years of age. In the USA, a prospective longitudinal study of older children placed in the Casey long-term foster care programme (Pecora et al, 1998) found the same rate of placement breakdown (around 50 per cent) that Thoburn and Rowe (1991) found for adoptive and permanent foster placements in the UK of children placed when aged 11 or older.

Smaller-scale studies provide contradictory findings. The placement breakdown rates reported by Berridge and Cleaver (1987) for long-term foster placements are similar to those reported by Thoburn and Rowe (1991) for children placed permanently with stranger adoptive or foster families. Gibbons and colleagues (1995) concluded from their study of children abused when they were under 5 years of age and followed up eight years later, that the well-being of those placed for adoption was no better than those in foster care, even though those in foster care had been placed later than those with adoptive families. However, long-term foster children who were subsequently adopted, when interviewed by Triseliotis and Russell (1984) and Hill and colleagues (1989) in a series of Scottish studies, came down firmly in favour of adoption. On a range of measures, the adopted young people were doing better than those brought up by long-term foster carers, and both were doing better than children brought up mainly in residential care.

Reporting on the first stage of a longitudinal study of long-term foster placements, Schofield and colleagues (2000) found that these are predominantly older children with complex family relationships and often traumatic backgrounds. Smaller-scale studies of young people 'ageing out' of stable foster family care at 18 and remaining in close touch with their foster families report satisfaction for young people and foster carers (Thoburn et al, 2000). The work of Stein (2000) suggests that most placements that last into adulthood are successful if measured against a range of criteria to indicate well-being. Sinclair and colleagues (2000) found that more than half of the 151 foster children who responded to their survey wished to remain with their foster families until age 18 or beyond.

The second group of children for whom more reliable outcome data are available are those placed with foster families not previously known to them (sometimes known as 'stranger placements'), with the clear intention that this will become a 'family for life'. They are often placed by specialist adoption and permanence teams, and placement practice differs little from adoption practice. Thoburn and Rowe (1991) and Thoburn and others (2000) found that around 20 per cent of 1,165 permanently placed children were permanently fostered (almost 30 per cent of the children who were of minority ethnic origin). When other variables were held constant, they found no difference in breakdown rates between those placed for adoption and those placed as permanent foster children. When other variables are considered, including satisfaction of the new parents and young people, findings vary and numbers are small. Thoburn (1990) found that the adopted and the permanent foster children were equally likely to have a 'sense of permanence', although some of the children chose to be adopted in their late teens.

What makes a good foster carer? Young people's views

These are the comments of three young people in foster care at a consultation event to inform the design of a new service, Fostering Adolescents in Merseyside (FAIM).

- 'They should be loving and understanding.'
- 'They should talk to you and show that they want to listen.'
- 'They should be able to compromise with the child – by saying things like "yes okay you can do this" on such and such day but then "I want you to do this" the next day – that way they can both get what they want and they are doing it in the right way instead of effing and blinding and arguing.'
- 'And they should talk to you about the future instead of pretending you are going to be in foster care all your life. Because I am moving out next year and my foster parents have talked to me about the future and what I am going to do. It means that they are not just dismissing me and once I go then they are not going to just forget who I am.'
- 'I think foster carers should be able to realise when kids are under stress and they need some time out so the foster carer needs to be able to say "you are doing too much; chill out and go out for the day and have a break so you don't get too stressed, get wound up and do something stupid".'
- 'They have got to take you places like on holiday, instead of leaving you behind. Because then it shows that they like being with you and stuff.'
- 'They don't have to be young – the older the wiser I think.'
- 'But it depends on the child – if a child feels more comfortable talking to a younger person then they should be with a younger type of foster parent. And if you feel comfortable talking to an older adult – then you stay with them. So it doesn't matter if they are young or old – it's whether or not you can get on with them.'
- 'They have to be friendly, outgoing; loves to have a laugh but knows when to stop as well.'
- 'Firm but fair.'
- 'Loving and understanding, talk to you and show that they want to listen and they care.'

Information on the success of kinship care

Kinship care, or care by relatives and friends with the agreement of the local authority, has been found to be more successful for the full range of children than placement with 'stranger' carers – those not previously known to the child. This evidence dates as far back in the UK as the work by Rowe and colleagues (1984) on long-term placement with relatives. They found that children fostered in this way seemed to be doing better on almost all counts than children in the care of those not previously known to them. This remains a rare study of outcomes in kinship care, though the numbers are small. The findings were replicated in the larger-scale study by Rowe and colleagues (1989) and by Berridge and Cleaver (1987) in their study of foster-home breakdowns.

The foreword to a collection of papers edited by Holman (1988) stated: 'Conventional wisdom tells us that such placements [with relatives] are likely to cause difficulties but this research study refutes the myth and demonstrates the enormous potential for all concerned.' This is something also borne out by Tunnard and Morris (1996). Jackson and Thomas (1999), reviewing what works in creating stability for looked-after children, said that 'placement with relatives' and 'placement with siblings' were among 'several factors' that 'strongly' made for stability in placements.

Kinship care has been officially encouraged through the UK for some time. Indeed in 1958 Manchester children's department had 44 per cent of its foster children in the care of relatives as against the then national average of 21 per cent (Holman, 2002). Guidance which accompanied the Children Act 1989, the Children (Scotland) Act 1995 and the Children (Northern Ireland) Order 1995 stated that local authorities should explore the possibility of children and young people being cared for by their family or people known to them before considering foster care by strangers. However, as Broad and colleagues (2001) say, this is 'largely invisible as a policy issue', adding what could be taken to be a natural consequence of this, that there is 'a dearth of information and much confusion surrounding its definition'.

The use of family and friends as carers varies between countries. In England, 17 per cent of looked-after children were in the care of relatives and friends in 2001, against 14.6 per cent in 1997 (Department of Health, 2002). In Wales nearly a fifth of children and young people (504 of 2,691 children) were cared for in this way at 31 March 2000 (Welsh Assembly, 2001). This is to be compared with Poland (90 per cent); New Zealand (75 per cent); the USA and Belgium (both 33 per cent) and Sweden (25 per cent) (Greeff, 1999).

However, it is difficult to interpret these figures since many children live with relatives but are not formally 'looked after'. Some local authorities have a policy of not accommodating children cared for by relatives (or of discharging care orders once children move to live with relatives), and, if necessary, supporting the placements through family support payments under Section 17 of the Children Act 1989 and other services or residence order allowances.

Thus comparisons between practice in different countries should be treated cautiously. Care takes place in very different contexts – for example, in the USA there is no financial support for families caring for a child in this way, unless the child is officially in care. But, that said, it is worth offering some comparisons and lessons from the other side of the Atlantic. For example, both Broad and others (2001) and the Child Welfare League of America (1994) found that half or nearly half of the carers in their samples were grandparents (50 per cent in the USA and 42 per cent in England). Half of Broad and colleagues' children and young people were black and of Caribbean and Guyanese origin, and in all but one case the ethnic origin of carer and child matched exactly. The higher percentages of black children cared for in this way may say something about cultural preferences.

Although they have stated that their sample of interviewees was too small to generalise from, Wheal and Waldeman (1999) note that 'it did seem that there were some problems regarding the lack of understanding or knowledge of social workers regarding family formations and cultural expectations'.

Greater stability was found to be a characteristic of kinship placements by both Broad and others (2001) in the UK, and the Child Welfare League of America (1994). In the UK, 46 per cent of the placements had lasted continuously for between one and five years and a third for more than five years. The administrative categories by which placements were made in the UK differed a lot – there were those under Section 17 of the Children Act 1989, while others were made on the basis of residence or care orders.

Children's views of kinship care

How children react to these placements depends on prior relationships with their carers, the age of the children and the situation in which they were living, as Wheal and Waldeman (1999) report. They also found that the presence of siblings eased the children's anxieties about separation – children who are cared for by friends and family are more likely to be cared for with their brothers and sisters than are other looked-after children. 'Emotional permanence' – feeling safe and secure living in their extended family – was something that the children felt from the love that they received, according to Broad and colleagues (2001).

The benefits children reported to Broad and colleagues (2001) included:

- stability
- avoiding local authority care and being looked after by people whom they did not know
- feeling safe in the company of adults
- maintaining links with family, brothers, sisters and friends
- sustaining their racial and cultural heritage
- being supported in their education.

Kosenson (1993), in a study in Scotland, found that children in kinship care were more likely to return to their families, after a period of care outside them. Brown and others (2002), who looked at 30 African-American young people living with family, found that they had extensive experience of living in this way prior to any formal arrangement being made. They recommend that service providers and researchers understand the adaptable and flexible nature of the family and acknowledge that this flexibility often protects families faced with social and economic adversity.

Another American study (Ehrle and Geen, 2002) found that children in kin arrangements faced greater handicaps, like poverty, than those who were in stranger foster care. They pointed out that (in the USA) 300,000 children lived in voluntary kinship care. They were of particular concern because they were not in the care of the state and, thus, might or might not be monitored by childcare agencies. In the UK there will be many children living with close relatives who are not the subject of formal arrangements. But there will be others who are privately fostered – that is, living with relatives not recognised by the law (those other than siblings, grandparents, step-parents, and aunts and uncles). They are most unlikely to be known to social workers (Philpot, 2001).

There are several studies that refer to kinship care: Lahti (1982), Fein and others (1983), Rowe and others (1984), Berridge and Cleaver (1987) and Barth and others (1994). All of these come to the same conclusions about the success of placing the full range of children with relatives or friends. Barth and others' (1994) study in the

USA found a lower level of disturbance among these children than among children in foster care with strangers. Other American researchers (Tesa and Slack, 2002), in a study of 93 children in kinship care in Cook County, Illinois, found that children whose parents were reported as regularly visiting and working towards regaining custody were more likely to be reunited and less likely to be replaced than children whose parents were reported to be uncooperative with visiting and service plans.

Relatives and friends have a particular advantage of being able to help the child with identity issues at the same time as providing a higher level of care than was available when the child was living with the birth parents. However, placement with relatives is becoming a placement of choice in a wider range of circumstances in the UK and America, and it may be that more risks will be taken and consequently the proportion of successful placements will decrease.

Carer's views of kinship care

Broad and colleagues (2001) found that kinship carers wanted support as much as did other carers. They were uncertain what they were entitled to, financially and otherwise, and they also wanted more information. Half of them felt isolated and lacking in support. As well as this and being poorly rewarded, and their homes being overcrowded, half of them were also struggling to cope with children exhibiting difficult behaviour. Earlier research by the National Foster Care Association (1993b) found that friends and relatives believed support from the local authority to be crucial in making placements a success.

Sykes and colleagues (2002) conducted a large-scale study in the US on kinship care, and found that it is a valued resource less well supported than care by strangers. Drawing on that data to see if similar issues arise in the UK, Sykes and colleagues (2002) conclude that:

- kinship carers are not a homogeneous group and they have different training needs, although some do not see themselves as being in need of training
- not all kinship carers want the support which is available to non-relative carers, but some do
- when kinship carers take on this responsibility they often suffer financially and in terms of their accommodation
- the potential for kinship care to 'unlock' support and help from grandparents and within minority ethnic communities is not sufficiently realised

- there may be particular difficulties for kinship carers when it comes to contact with birth families; this needs to be assessed before placement, and sympathetic social work support needs to be available thereafter.

Some of these conclusions and others are reached by Philpot and Broad (2003), who also make a number of policy recommendations.

Arguments about the preventative aspects of care by relatives were boosted by Richards' study for the Family Rights Group (Richards, 2001). She reported a survey of 180 grandparents who had taken over the care of their grandchildren. All of these children would otherwise have gone into local authority care, unless another relative had stepped in. The grandparents often had to fight in court for their grandchildren and the courts would not have supported the grandparents if the parents had been in a position to provide good enough care.

Kinship carers are, in important respects, a special kind of carer, but they are not a homogenous group. They have their own needs and a view of their capacities but in many ways they share many characteristics with stranger foster carers, and both groups voice many of the same complaints about lack of support and express many of the same needs.

Decision-making and adoptive families

The most reliable information on outcomes concerns adoptive placements. Overall, findings from available research show that when we look at whether the placement did not break down within a period of five or more years, whatever the route to permanence chosen, the age of the child at placement appears to be the key variable. Below the age of 11, the younger the child at placement, the more likely it is that the placement will be successful on all measures.

In addition to increasing age, other variables significantly associated with placement breakdown include being emotionally or behaviourally disturbed at the time of placement, and having been maltreated or neglected prior to placement (Thoburn, 1991). Others identify being 'singled out' for rejection by the birth parents (Quinton et al, 1998), or having experienced multiple moves, as associated with placement breakdown or lower well-being, but the information that we have here is less robust. Having two black or Asian parents does not appear to be associated with placement breakdown, although Thoburn and Rowe (1991) found that children of mixed-race parentage were more likely to have disrupted placements than white children or those with two parents of minority ethnic origin.

This section now looks in detail at the information and research evidence available on the adoption of children of different ages (infants, and older children) and the impact of other biographical factors on the outcome of placements. It then looks at long-term placement and continued contact with birth relatives, children from black and minority ethnic groups, and explores different findings on experiences and preferences for adoption, long-term fostering or residence orders.

The adoption of infants

Few workers today are involved in the placement of infants (children less than 1 year old) whose parents have requested an adoption placement. However, there are increasing numbers of placements of children removed from their parents at birth or shortly after and placed, usually for adoption, which are contested by their parents.

It can be estimated from Neil's (2000a; 2000b) longitudinal research on children adopted from care when under 4 years of age that fewer than 300 babies are voluntarily relinquished in England each year and even in these cases adoption may be complex. She found that of 62 children placed when under the age of 12 months, only 23 (37 per cent) were relinquished infants; 34 per cent were more complex cases but not contested in court; and 29 per cent were adopted from care against parental wishes.

These figures are congruent with the Department of Health's statistics. In 2002, 3,600 of the 58,700 children and young people looked after by English local authorities were placed with their prospective adopters and only 240 of these were under 1 year of age (Department of Health, 2003). Of the 1,600 children looked after whose legal status was 'freed for adoption', only 130 (7 per cent) were aged under 12 months. When we look at the 3,400 children actually adopted during 2001/02, 190 were adopted when under the age of 12 months. Although 1,900 of the 3,400 had started to be looked after when under the age of 1, only 210 were actually adopted within 12 months (Department of Health, 2003).

Although some of the 'delayed adoptions' of infants will result from poor practice, many of them will be the 'complex' adoptions referred to by Neil (2000b), including adoption from care where consent has to be dispensed with. The Department of

Health statistics show that a third of children for whom adoption is the plan are adopted within two years of entering local authority care, and the majority are adopted within five years. While 8 per cent waited for five years, most of these children were adopted by foster parents with whom they may have been living for some time.

Although it is not hard to find families for infants, the nature of the information given to the child as he or she grows up can be complex and such placements have not to our knowledge been evaluated nor described as a separate group in the recent literature. Thus, we know little about how new parents talk to children about, for example, the fact that their father killed their mother, that their mother had a severe mental illness or that they were removed from their mother at birth because she had a tendency to live with unsafe men and previous children had been sexually abused. Nor do we know from research whether attempts are made to help these children to get in touch with siblings placed in foster or adoptive homes, perhaps before they were born. It seems likely that it is assumed that such children are 'easy to place' and therefore placed by area team social workers or more traditional adoption agencies. From the available research, it appears that the post-placement needs of these children and their carers are being under-estimated.

Concurrent planning, as a strategy to avoid delay in placement has been widely adopted since the Children Act 1989, reinforced by the local authority circular LAC 98 (20). It involves doing preliminary work on a contingency care plan in case the preferred plan is unsuccessful. In a more specific sense, concurrent planning refers to a model of practice that has been imported to the UK from the USA. The aim is to reduce the amount of time children spend in temporary placements, and to reduce the number of moves between families before a permanent placement is agreed. The agency runs two plans concurrently. First, every effort is made to rehabilitate the child with his or her birth family. To that end, the problems that prevent the birth parents from providing a safe and nurturing environment for the child are assessed, and they are supported in addressing those problems on a timescale (for example, six months) that makes sense in a child's terms. Meanwhile, under the second plan the foster family has also been assessed and matched as an adoptive family, and will adopt the child if the first plan fails. This family operates as a foster family until the care plan is determined at the final hearing, and the foster carers are expected to support arrangements with the birth parents.

There are descriptive but as yet no published evaluation studies of this model of practice in the USA (Katz et al, 1994). In the UK, it is in its infancy, with only three projects currently: in Manchester, Brighton and London. These projects are described and evaluated by Monck and colleagues (2003). According to Gray (2002), it will be 'several years' before the long-term outcomes for the children from present projects become available. In the USA this pattern of work is expected to provide for children up to 8 years old. In the three UK projects the children have been very young, and half were placed at birth with the concurrent carers. This makes it possible for the children in contested cases to start to live with prospective adopters at an earlier stage and with fewer moves than experienced by similar children in mainstream care cases.

One of the most contentious aspects of these projects concerns contact between birth child and birth parent. Contact is offered as frequently as possible because to do otherwise would be to the detriment of child and birth parents if return to the birth family proved possible. It is also intended that contact will promote attachment and make return to the birth family more likely. Initially, the parents and their child may be offered maximum contact of three times a week but practitioners disagree about whether this is too frequent, perhaps especially as the proportions of children actually leaving adopters to join birth parents are very small. However, contact arrangements are settled in court and it is very unlikely that the court would believe it was right to be guided by such probabilities.

There is a substantial body of knowledge about the outcomes for infants placed at birth or shortly afterwards at the request of their parents. However, much of this research is now dated and concerns practice that may have changed. Generally it concludes that around 5 per cent of these placements will be unsuccessful in the sense that the child and adoptive family will part company and the adoptive parents will not function as a 'family for life' for the adult adoptee. However, on other measures, including the satisfaction of the adopters and the adopted person, the conclusion from a range of studies is that around 80 per cent of adopters and adopted adults express satisfaction with their relationship, and around 20 per cent are generally dissatisfied (McWhinnie, 1967; Raynor, 1980).

When people are placed as babies in closed adoptions (where they have no contact with members of the birth family), one hazard found has been that a proportion of them develop emotional problems as teenagers and adults, regarding identity (Howe and Feast, 2000). However, there are indications that the risks associated with placement increase once a child is older than 6 months (Howe, 1992).

Similar rates of satisfaction and breakdown appear to apply to specific groups of children adopted as infants, including those with disabilities (Macaskill, 1985a); those placed from overseas, and those placed transracially (who may also be from overseas) (Gill and Jackson, 1983). However, when difficulties do arise with transracially placed children, these tend to be concentrated around issues of race, racism and black identity. Such difficulties tend to become more marked in the teenage years (Thoburn et al, 2000).

Rutter and colleagues (1998) have reported on early findings from a longitudinal study of Romanian adopted children, many of whom experienced adverse circumstances in their very early weeks and months. Although the full picture will not be available until the children reach adulthood, it is clear that most catch up quickly on physical development but some continue to have difficulties with social relationships. The major studies of inter-country adoption are Dutch and Scandinavian. Breakdown rates are similar to those described above, but a higher proportion of young children adopted from overseas entered residential care in Holland than would have been expected in the population of children who had not been adopted (Hoksbergen, 1986, 1991; Alstein and Simon, 1991). These children and their adoptive parents tackle, with varying degrees of success, the issue of mixed racial and cultural identity and the Scandinavian accounts are helpful in giving detailed information about the attitudes of the young adults as well as those of their adopters. (The earlier studies are summarised in the review of research relevant to adoption prepared by the Adoption Law Review (Department of Health, 1992), and by Selman and Wells (1996).

More recent studies on the placement of infants relate to North America, New Zealand and Canada, and concentrate on the issue of continued contact with members of the birth family. The early conclusions are that there are advantages to be gained from continuing contact for the children, the birth parents and the adopters. The nature and extent of contact varies from the exchange of letters to weekly meetings, though indirect contact is more common. The nature of contact also varies over time (McRoy, 1991). Most UK studies of attitudes of adopters are small-scale. Adopters as a group tend to be less enthusiastic about contact with birth parents, according to Owen (1996). Ryburn (1997), Thoburn and colleagues (2000) and Neil (2000) conclude that those children who have face-to-face contact with birth parents usually find it helpful. There is some evidence from New Zealand that, as such contact becomes the norm, public opinion is getting used to the idea that continuing contact is part of adoption.

In Britain the survey of adoption agencies reported by Joan Fratter and colleagues (1991) indicates that it is now quite usual for adopters and birth parents to meet before placement. Continuing direct contact is less common, but with the requirement in the Children Act that the wishes and feelings of parents should be consulted and due consideration given to them, it seems likely that more parents will request some form of continuing contact when their children are placed as infants with new parents. Lowe and others (1999) report that most adoption agencies and local authorities now provide a post-box service to facilitate indirect contact and the updating of information. It is possible that, when infants are placed early as part of a concurrent planning scheme (see above), the contact that is established early in the placement will continue if it is decided that the adoption will be proceeded with. The length of time over which concurrent-planning carers and birth parents had frequent contact made it possible at times to establish reasonably friendly relationships. This did not always happen, and in some cases birth parents – for a variety of reasons – failed completely to keep up contact sessions. It appeared that courts may have taken some account of these factors in settling future contacts.

Studies summarised by Brodzinsky and Schechter (1990), in an important book on the psychology of adoption, indicate that when adopted children and young adults do have problems related to their adoption, these often involve issues of identity. These authors follow Kirk (1965) in concluding that successful adoptive parenting of children placed as infants is associated with the ability to accept the child's dual identity and the emotional significance which the family of origin will always have for the child and for themselves as new parents. Kirk writes of the balance to be drawn between their acceptance of the challenge of adoptive parenting as a different sort of parenting, and the importance of not over-emphasising the difference.

Much has been learned from adults who have sought counselling under Section 51 of the Adoption Act 1976 before tracing birth relatives, and several small-scale studies report on this work (for example, Walby and Symons, 1990; Howe and Hinings, 1989; Howe and Feast, 2000). The main studies of young people who trace their birth relatives or seek additional information indicate that this form of searching is not usually associated with the young person having problems around the adoption, but rather results from natural curiosity and a wish to know more about their genetic make-up (Haimes and Timms, 1985; Howe and Feast, 2000).

The research on the outcomes for the birth parents of placing a child for adoption mainly concerns birth mothers, and little is known about the impact on birth fathers. The work of the Post-Adoption Centre, as reported by Howe and colleagues (1992), indicates that a substantial proportion of young women who gave up their children for adoption regretted doing so and suffered a range of emotionally disturbing symptoms well into their adult lives. In developed societies very few young women now choose adoption as a solution to the problem of an initially unwanted pregnancy. Neil's (2000) study indicates that birth parents and relatives who continue to have face-to-face contact after adoption find it is a positive and helpful experience, a conclusion matching those from the larger-scale American studies summarised by Grotevant and McRoy (1998).

Finally, then, to conclude this section on the adoption of infants, it is important to say that we do not know how these findings compare with the generality of children brought up by their parents, nor would it be easy to find a reference group given that adoptive parents are mostly chosen because they appear to be stable, competent and, in general terms, successful adults. On the question of age generally when considering adoption, although the numbers of children being adopted from care are rising, the numbers placed for adoption when over the age of 5 are falling. It would be unfortunate if the drive to place more children for adoption led to a focus on the youngest (and easiest to place) children at the expense of the majority of children who are over 5 when they start to be looked after.

Adoption for older children

Although numbers have risen in recent years, only a small proportion of the children who are admitted to care or are accommodated go on to need long-term or permanent placements. Roger Bullock and colleagues (1993) have estimated that 90 per cent will go home or return as teenagers to live in their home communities. Only 16 (3 per cent) of the 450 children who came into care in the cohort study by Millham and colleagues (1986) were adopted or placed with permanent long-term foster carers. Jane Rowe and colleagues (1989) found that long-term placements accounted for nearly one in ten of all foster placements and that only 3 per cent of over 10,000 placements studied were directly for adoption or with a view to adoption.

Department of Health statistics indicate that this proportion has gone up, but no large cohort studies of children entering care are yet available to replicate the Millham and Rowe studies.

The children in placement prior to being adopted form only a small proportion of the total population of children looked after. Department of Health statistics (2003a; 2003b) show that of the 59,700 children being looked after in March 2002, only 6 per cent (3,600) were in adoptive placements (although some of the nearly 38,400 foster placements may have been made prior to adoption or with long-term foster carers who may at some point go on to adopt). In the course of the year, 3,400 looked-after children in England were adopted. This includes around 14 per cent adopted by their foster carers. Of those adopted by their foster carers, around half were aged 10 or over and most of these will have been living with their foster carers for several years. While 42 per cent of children who were under 3 when they started to be looked after were adopted within two years of coming into care, this applied to only 15 per cent of those who were 3 or over when they started to be looked after.

Around 20 per cent of those adopted had been accommodated before the order was made and the remaining children were the subjects of care orders or freed for adoption. The number freed for adoption in recent years has doubled, while the number accommodated has gone down. Although the numbers and the proportion of children placed for adoption from care have gone up in recent years, the proportions and absolute numbers of those placed for adoption when aged 4 or more (leaving out those adopted by foster carers with whom they were placed when under 5) have gone down (Department of Health, 2001a).

Another big change brought about by the Children Act 1989 is the requirement to consult children, parents and close relatives on their wishes about the nature of the placement, and give due consideration to what they have to say. As a result there are more requests for placements where there will be continued contact with the birth family. In some cases where it is concluded that the child cannot be adequately protected from future harm (for example, where an older sibling has been abused by the mother's cohabitee whose continuing presence in the household is the main reason why the child cannot return home) there may, nevertheless, be a good attachment between the mother and child (Thoburn, 1996). In such cases a long-term placement may be needed where there is 'dual psychological parenting' over a transitional period or even until the child grows up.

Several UK and American studies of the placement of older children from care with new families have come up with remarkably similar results in terms of breakdown rates. A survey of 1,165 placements made by UK voluntary agencies between 1980 and 1985 concluded that one in five broke down within five years of placement (Thoburn and Rowe, 1991). A similar rate of breakdown was found by the Lothian family placement team (Triseliotis, 1991; Borland et al, 1991) and by Barth and Berry (1988), reviewing American research.

If other measures of outcome are considered, the success rate is likely to be lower since some placements continue even though they are considered less than satisfactory. However, work by Howe (1996) suggests that what might appear to be an unsatisfactory outcome, when the child has burst angrily out of the family home between the ages of 16 and 18, may look more positive when the young person is in their mid-20s and has managed to renegotiate a place in the adoptive family albeit from a separate base as a young adult. It may be that outcome of adoptions for children placed from care should not be measured until the young person is in their late 20s because there are so many additional obstacles to growing up to be overcome when a person has started life under adverse circumstances and then had to cope with the special issues around separation, placement in care and adoption.

Working together for older children and new families

Eight local authorities and several voluntary agencies make up the West Yorkshire Family Placement Consortium, with one of the voluntary agencies hosting meetings to provide a consistent base for meetings. The consortium identifies its keys to success as:

- membership of managers (usually assistant directors)
- appointing a dedicated worker to facilitate the consortium
- joint training
- reciprocal working arrangements, such as chairing each other's disruption meetings.

The right of a consortium to retain details of families for a further three months (beyond the three months for a single authority) has increased the commitment to joint working, as it rewards good use of local resources and increases the chances of placing children in families identified, supported and trained in West Yorkshire.

Within the consortium, the Barnardo's New Families Yorkshire service has found that its strength lies in adoption work. It brings a different dimension to the consortium by recruiting, preparing and supporting adopters for children who have traditionally been seen as hard to place, including children: who need to be placed as a sibling group, from black and minority ethnic backgrounds, who are disabled, who are older or have had multiple placements.

Age at placement and other biographical factors

Many studies emphasise the importance of the age of a child at the time of placement. Once over the age of 6 months, the vulnerability to emotional problems around attachment has been found to increase with age at placement (Howe, 1996; Fratter et al, 1991; Thoburn and Rowe, 1991). There is consistency among findings from several studies that around one in ten of those placed with new parents not previously known to them at the age of 5, around one in five of those aged 7 or 8 at placement, and almost half of 11- or 12-year-olds will experience breakdown of their 'permanent' placement, whether this is in an adoptive or a permanent foster family.

Within these broad age bands, researchers have highlighted other vulnerability factors. Children who have physical or learning disabilities generally do as well or better when placed with new parents than children who in other respects are similar (Gath, 1983; Macaskill, 1985a; Wolkind and Kazuruk, 1986; Thoburn et al, 1986; Argent, 1998; Fratter et al, 1991). Children described as institutionalised, having behavioural or emotional difficulties, being placed away from siblings, and having a history of abuse or neglect all have greater risks of experiencing breakdown of placements, according to the study by Thoburn and Rowe (1991), which is large enough for these variables to be held constant. This study concludes that while difficult past experiences, such as several moves in temporary foster care, are not factors independently associated with breakdown, children who suffer behavioural and emotional difficulties, including a lack of trust in adults, are more likely to be found among those whose earlier placements have broken down. The inference can be drawn that placement instability prior to joining the new family is a relevant factor if it has led to emotional and behavioural problems.

Gibbons and colleagues' (1995) conclusion that abused or neglected children often continue to experience difficulties when placed with new families finds echoes in the conclusion of the Thoburn and Rowe study (1991) that those who had been abused or neglected were more likely to experience placement breakdown. Most of the studies described in this report concern a group of children of which the majority have been exposed to parental maltreatment. Although some of the qualitative studies comment on individuals or sub-groups who have been exposed to different types of abuse, such as sexual abuse or physical assault, the overlap between the types of abuse and the generally small numbers means that any conclusions drawn remain tentative.

Some commentators writing about sexually abused children, or about children of parents who have killed a family member, argue that such cases should be considered differently, especially in terms of continuing contact with the abusing or neglectful parents. The research is not there to back these assertions or to contradict them.

Contact with birth relatives

Continuing contact between adopted children and members of their birth family is found in some studies to be associated with a reduced risk of breakdown, and appears to make no difference in others. Thoburn and Rowe (1991), find a statistically significant association for 1,165 children surveyed between the child having face-to-face contact with a parent after placement and the placement lasting for at least five years. This finding is particularly important since the cohort was large enough for variables, such as age at placement and behaviour difficulties, to be held constant. Fratter (1996) found from a small qualitative study that although not all the adopters welcomed contact, the open adoptions she studied were generally successful and that the contact was not seen by parents or children as a reason for the problems which some of them experienced. Aldgate (1990), Berridge and Cleaver (1987), Barth and Berry (1988), Borland and colleagues (1991) and Kelly (1995) found similarly with adoption and long-term foster placements.

Macaskill (2002) researched the experience of post-placement contact with birth families in a sample of 76 long-term foster carers and adoptive parents and their 106 children. The sources of information were mainly social workers and records. The children had been placed between 1960 and 1999 and were aged from 5 to over 18. Fifty-two adoptive parents and foster carers and 37 young people were interviewed. It was concluded that, despite a range of difficulties experienced by some of them, 'children were resolute in their wish to see their birth relatives'. Thoburn and colleagues (2000) found similarly with those children of minority ethnic origin who continued to see their birth parents. Macaskill builds on her research to make recommendations about practice with birth parents, adoptive parents and foster carers to make contact a more positive experience.

A Social Services Inspectorate report (Department of Health, 1995d) gives a picture of the extent of direct and indirect post-adoption contact in 37 adoption agencies in the North of England. Neil and colleagues (forthcoming) discuss the similarities and differences between birth-family contact in long-term foster care and in adoption. An academic 'debate' discussing the key findings is to be found in Quinton and colleagues (1997), Ryburn (1997) and Quinton and Selwyn (1998).

Being placed with one or more siblings is found in some studies to be associated with more successful outcomes (Fratter et al, 1991; Wedge and Mantle, 1991). Neil (1999), Dance and Rushton (1999) and Rushton and colleagues (2001) have summarised the evidence on the importance of placing children with new families who can either keep looked-after brothers and sisters together, or ensure that they continue to have comfortable contact with each other. Rushton and colleagues (2001) describe the characteristics, pre-placement experience and first 12 months in their new families of 133 children in sibling groups, some placed together, some 'split'(in two different places) and some 'splintered'(in three or more places). This is the first stage of a detailed and complex longitudinal study. At this stage, there can be only pointers to assist practice in making decisions about placing brothers and sisters together or separately, but there is nothing to date to contradict other studies that have indicated that being placed with a brother or sister will usually be a protective factor.

Children from black and minority ethnic groups

The ethnic origin of the child is another factor that has gained the attention of researchers. Rowe and colleagues (1989) argue that it is important to disaggregate groups of black and minority ethnic children. Thoburn and Rowe (1991) found from their large-scale survey that children whose birth parents were both black or Asian were no more likely to experience placement breakdowns than children whose birth parents were both white, but that children of mixed ethnicity were more likely to be in placements that disrupted.

They also found that children whose birth parents were both black or Asian were more likely to be placed with a sibling, to remain in contact with a sibling placed elsewhere, and to be in contact with their birth parents than was the case with either the white children or the black children of mixed racial parentage. For children in short- as well as long-term foster care, we have previously referred to the work of Barn and the research she summarises when looking at these issues (see the section on 'Race and ethnicity' in Chapter 2).

June Thoburn and colleagues (2000) scrutinised the records of 297 children of minority ethnic origin (mainly drawn from the earlier study) between six and eleven years after placement with adoptive or (for a third of them) permanent foster families. Just over two-thirds were placed with white families. A purposive sample of 51 of the young people was identified and 24 of them and 38 adoptive parents or foster carers were interviewed when the young people were aged between 11 and 30. The interview sample was selected to include equal numbers placed in ethnically matched families and placed with white families. The number of black and Asian children who reach adulthood having been permanently placed in culturally and racially matched families in the UK is still small and therefore little research evidence is yet available on the long-term outcomes for these children. Thoburn and colleagues found no statistically significant difference in placement breakdown rates whether the child and new parents were of similar or different origin.

There is general agreement between UK and American researchers that some white parents, especially those who live in ethnically mixed communities, can successfully parent black children (Ladner, 1977; McRoy et al, 1982; Gill and Jackson, 1983; Shireman and Johnson, 1986; Howe, 1996). Barth (1988) found no difference in disruption rates between transracial and same-race placements. However, qualitative studies (Ince, 1998; Thoburn et al, 2000; Kirton, 2000; Kirton et al, 2000) provide evidence that some young people consider that they have lost out by being placed transracially. When parents and children are visibly different, there are extra obstacles to overcome in adapting to adoptive family life, and white families have additional difficulties and challenges to overcome in ensuring that black children have a positive sense of their racial and cultural identity.

Most of the UK writing on this subject tends to use service outcome measures and focuses on the success or otherwise of attempts to recruit black families and to achieve same-race placements (Small, 1986; Barn, 1993b). Much of it is in the form of descriptive accounts by practitioners but the literature does demonstrate that agencies determined to recruit new black parents succeed in doing so. Caesar and colleagues (1994) describe an important Barnardo's initiative to provide 'professional' permanent new families for older children who have serious behavioural and emotional problems. They particularly focus on the success of the project in recruiting black families who, from the descriptive accounts, appear to be providing high-quality care.

More recent studies (Ivaldi, 2000; Neil, 2000a), as well as the Department of Health statistics, indicate that it is now unusual for children with two black or Asian parents to be placed with white families, although children with one black or Asian grandparent are still as likely as not to be placed with a white family.

CASE STUDY 5

Inclusive working with black and minority ethnic staff and service users

In 2001/02, over half of the children placed by the Bradford-based Barnardo's New Families Yorkshire Project were placed with adopters from black and Asian communities. A well-regarded, professional and dynamic worker from an Asian community is clearly an asset to this project but the project could not have this level of success in placing black and minority ethnic children in appropriate placements if that appointment was merely tokenistic. Joint working of assessments within the project means that overall expertise in working appropriately with Asian service users has increased.

The service has invested in an Urdu computer package enabling translation of literature. Signs in and around the project are in community languages, signalling the inclusive approach of the project. Likewise, although the project has used direct advertising, it is wary of one-off targeted recruitment drives which can appear tokenistic. Analysis of recent recruitment demonstrates that the most successful response comes from word-of-mouth contact with people who have already used the service.

In West Yorkshire, the Family Placement Consortium has been instrumental in facilitating the development of a successful Asian workers' sub-group which operates and links workers across the consortium. Asian practitioners share resources and skills and have developed joint preparatory training for prospective adopters from Asian communities.

Fostering, adoption or residence orders?

Lowe and Murch with others (2002) have explored the reasons why long-term foster-family care is the placement of choice (or becomes so when adoption plans fail to work out) for some children, and adoption for others. The age of the child, contact arrangements and the nature of relationships with the birth family (including the need to be placed with a sibling) are major determinants alongside the availability of families. Long-term foster children who were subsequently adopted came down firmly in favour of adoption when interviewed by Triseliotis and Russell (1984) and Hill and colleagues (1989) in a series of Scottish studies. This is the conclusion that Triseliotis (2002) comes to when comparing adoption with long-term foster care. He concludes from a review of research that the defining differences between the two kinds of placement are the higher levels of emotional security, sense of belonging and general well-being expressed by those who grew up adopted compared with those who grew up in long-term foster care.

This is an area where researchers and commentators disagree about the conclusions to be drawn, possibly because of the different research samples informing their conclusions. Some researchers who have focused on outcomes of long-term or permanent foster placements (Schofield, 2003; Thoburn, 1990; Thoburn et al, 2000) conclude that it is possible for long-term foster children and their foster carers to have a sense of permanence and emotional security that allows the young adults to remain part of the family. Triseliotis concurs with other authors that decisions about where to place children have to take account of their individual needs and circumstances and those of their carers. Nor, he adds, is adoption the answer for every child ('the same shoe cannot fit every foot'). Long-term fostering, he asserts, still has a 'firm' place in planning.

Several writers have noted that there is a group of mainly older children who would not allow themselves to be placed with substitute families if they had to break close links with their families of origin, and foster placement rather than adoption is likely to be more appropriate for these children. In a study of custodianship, Bullard and Malos (1991) identified a group of children who wished to leave care, but did not want to be adopted, for whom custodianship (now residence order) was appropriate. It appears that birth parents whose children are removed against their wishes usually but not always prefer a legal status for their children of 'permanent fostering' or a residence order, although more research is needed on this.

CASE STUDY 6

Giving children security in foster care

Mrs H has been fostering since 1996. She had raised her own children to adulthood, knew someone who was already fostering and decided that she wanted to do more. Two children, aged 4 and 6, were placed with her in 1997. She says that it was a rough ride at first, partly due to a negative reaction from the children's birth grandmother. Mrs H attends monthly group meetings of foster carers who meet to share problems, support each other and discuss issues.

'Every kid is an individual,' she says 'and just because I go through a rough patch it doesn't mean you will.' She would advise people to seek help from their social worker, discuss problems early and ask for the best available information for foster carers in advance of a placement being made.

Mrs H has recently started attending a course on managing children's behaviour. 'It does help with it, I don't know if it's a generation thing or the individual or whether they distance themselves. Some of the kids, because they've been moved about so many times, they think "well I'm not getting close, because I will be moved again". I had to tell them "This is your home, you're staying"'.

CASE STUDY 7

Adoption or fostering? 'It's what's best for her'

Several years ago Ms J fostered a 6-year-old girl, with a view to adoption. As the foster daughter grew older, she began to say that she didn't want to be adopted. To maintain continuity, the placement has become a long-term foster placement instead.

'People doing this may need to compromise because in the end it's about what's best for her, because she has us, and she knows that's forever but she knows that there's that window, that if her birth mum is ever strong enough she can have contact.

'We [foster mother and fostering service] haven't always seen eye to eye, but I think what they have said has always been in our interest. We have both wanted my daughter to be happy but sometimes we have been coming at it in two different ways. They have let her express her views and have written her views into the plans.'

Ms J has a birth daughter of similar age, 'The two girls didn't get on at first but there was no way she wasn't staying; when my foster daughter came into the house it was forever, it wasn't negotiable.'

Parents also vary in their views of different kinds of long-term placements. While it appears that most potential long-term carers of younger children prefer adoption, there is a range of views among those offering to care permanently for older children with special needs. Some of those interviewed by researchers prefer the child to remain in care, in part so that they can be sure of continuing social work support. Thoburn and colleagues (2000) found that a higher proportion of the black and Asian new families were permanent foster families than was the case for white or mixed-race partnerships. This was associated with higher levels of contact with birth parents and sibling when children were placed with black or Asian parents.

The special guardianship orders under the Adoption and Children Act 2002 are intended to provide permanence and security throughout childhood to children for whom adoption is not suitable, and to remove them from the status of being 'looked after'. Whether and how these aims are achieved will demand the attention of future research.

In summary, there is insufficient evidence on the desirability of adoption, permanent fostering or residence orders, from the child's point of view. There is, however, evidence that the generally negative view of long-term or 'permanent' foster care is not supported by recent research. There appear to be no differences in terms of breakdown rates, and the evidence on well-being and satisfaction of children and new parents is inconclusive.

It is important for practitioners to look closely at the results of qualitative as well as quantitative studies to help them to decide which is likely to work best for each particular child or sibling group. Interviews with adopters and adopted young people in the above studies and in the study of Thomas and Beckford with others (1999), Thoburn and others (2000) and Hill and others (1989) provide helpful clues. For some children, only adoption and for others only foster placement will be acceptable. For some, legal status is much less important than finding a family who can empathise with the child's earlier life and facilitate the appropriate form of contact with birth parents and siblings. In such circumstances, the outcome research would support a twin-track approach looking concurrently for either an adoptive or a foster family, thus widening the pool of potential families and decreasing the delay caused by starting to look for foster carers only after months or even years have elapsed and no adopters have been found.

'One day she rang me at work, asking me what did she need to do to become adopted. So I contacted the social worker. She knew I wanted to adopt her, but I felt adoption was a

two-way thing. It wasn't something I wanted to do to her. I got our social worker to come round and she spent some time talking to her on her own about it. Initially, her mum refused to sign the adoption papers and then she agreed to sign in the end. I think it was the right thing for me to adopt – not only for her but also for me. I would not like it if I died tomorrow for anybody to come and challenge her about anything as my daughter.'
FOSTER CARER WHO WENT ON TO ADOPT

'They asked me about adopting Clive, and I said no. Clive's daddy loved him in his own way and he had a link with his dad, and it would have meant a lot of changes, and I don't think it would have been fair to rob him [the birth father] of someone that he had loved in his own way.'
AFRICAN-CARIBBEAN FOSTER CARER

'The social worker said it was drift – she should be adopted. The mother wanted her fostered. She [fostered child] never wanted to take our name. She wanted her own name. We had to fight the mother and the local authority on the custodianship order.'
FOSTER CARER WHO WENT ON TO ADOPT

The evidence for effective practice

Because of the complexities affecting adoption and other long-term placements, few researchers have been able to relate specific aspects of practice to specific outcomes. However, most describe the work in some detail, and, insofar as specific methods are practised in agencies with reasonably good results, it is possible to take messages for practice from the research writing. Fratter and colleagues (1991), for example, found that disruption rates for different voluntary agencies placing similar children varied between 10 per cent and 50 per cent. A detailed description of the practice of an agency with only 10 per cent of placements of older children disrupted within five years of placement ought to produce useful information about the sort of practice which might lead to successful placements (Thoburn et al, 1986). Rushton et al (1995) describe the different models of practice of the children's workers and conclude that these differences had an impact on whether the adopters were able to surmount the difficulties they encountered

Rushton and colleagues (2001) have made the most comprehensive study of practice with adoptive parents or foster carers and children around the time of placement. When reviewing case histories a year after placement, they concluded: 'In the cases of positive outcome it was impossible to say whether it was the intervention itself, the efforts of the [adoptive] parents [and foster carers], the passage of time, or a combination of factors that made the difference' (Rushton et al, 2001, p145). Most of the studies already cited provide 'service outcome' data in that they describe the types of services provided at the various stages. The study by Lowe and colleagues (1999) is particularly useful and draws out some differences between practice in the voluntary and local authority sectors. Most of the smaller studies provide information on satisfaction (mainly of adopters) with different aspects of the service. Thomas and Beckford with others (1999) provide compelling evidence on the views of 41 recently adopted children (mostly aged between 8 and 12) about the whole adoption process.

In reviewing the evidence for a Quality Protects research briefing, Thoburn (2002a) summarises what is known about services to adoptive families, children and young people, and birth parents. Many of the messages echo those already reported above for short-term placements. Perhaps the strongest message is that clear and accurate information should be provided at all stages to birth parents, new parents and (in an age-appropriate way) children. Since continuing direct or indirect contact is now a feature of most permanent arrangements, the evidence provided by Neil (2002a) is also relevant. She found that the why and the how of contact were not adequately covered in the recruitment and training of adopters.

Effective recruitment and retention of permanent new parents

Recruitment

The research on what makes for good results is clearly relevant when recruiting permanent new parents. Outcome studies have usually considered whether any particular characteristics of the new parents appear to be associated with more or less successful placements. Most of the main studies already referred to have something to say about placement practice. Therefore, individual sources are listed only when they make a very specific point or diverge from the conclusions of the majority.

There is one variable that consistently appears to be a factor in the placement of infants as well as older children as a risk factor – if the new family has a child close in age to the child to be placed. Qualitative data from surveys and interviews indicate that the new brothers and sisters of adopted children within new families can be either a source of support or can be distressed or even harmed by the placement (for example, Thoburn, 1990; Pugh, 1996; Lowe et al, 1999).

Otherwise, research studies differ in their findings about the sorts of people who can successfully become new parents for children who have suffered some form of adversity before placement. Most studies find that more experienced and older parents are more successful, but some have found that younger childless couples have been particularly successful, especially with groups of siblings (Hart, 1986; Barth, 1988; Wedge and Mantle, 1991; Rushton et al, 2001). Larger families with grown-up children and relatives able to provide additional support tend to be well represented among those who are successful (Thoburn et al, 1986).

Moving away from these more obvious characteristics, writers agree about the attitudes, personality characteristics and skills of new parents who are more successful (Nelson 1986; Thoburn et al, 1986). It appears to be important that they enjoy a challenge, and that they enjoy spending time with children. Some studies have associated religious faith and church attendance with successful parenting of children who are older and who have special needs (Nelson, 1985). There are also indications from the research about the characteristics and skills of parents who are most likely to be successful with a child with a learning disability (Macaskill, 1985a; Gath, 1983) or those who are behaviourally or emotionally disturbed (Macaskill, 1985b; Thoburn et al, 1986; Rushton et al, 1988; 1995; 2001). Determination and enjoying a challenge figure highly on all these lists.

The psychology of adoption research (Brodzinsky and Schechter, 1990) suggests that it is important for new parents to feel comfortable about integrating a child's early history into their family life. It is especially important that they can understand and make a good attempt to empathise with the parent who was responsible for the maltreatment, or who was unable to protect the child from it. A child whose parent is known to have abused him or her is likely to need support in establishing a positive sense of self and this will not be helped if the adopters or foster carers make it clear that they have a low opinion or condemnatory attitude towards the birth parents.

Where the recruitment of permanent new parents differs from that of short-term and intermediate carers is that the matching process is a second opportunity to decide whether a child should be placed even after the family has been formally approved. Once a short-term and intermediate carer is approved it is almost certain that at least one short-term or intermediate placement will be made. However, it is possible to be more adventurous about the recruitment process for permanent families since a child will not be placed unless the family seems 'right' for a particular child. Studies make clear that a very wide range of single people or couples have successfully parented children who have experienced difficulties in their early lives or are disabled.

Permanent-placement workers in specialist agencies all report that some of the most successful new parents were originally rejected when they applied to local authorities or adoption agencies concentrating on the placement of infants. Caine (1992) undertook a consumer study of 'unusual' adopters who applied to a Barnardo's project, and Owen (1996) studied 30 single-parent adopters. Despite the complex problems of the 48 children placed with them, these placements appeared to be working well both for the children and adopters. Eleven of these parents were black. Both of these studies provide encouragement for the practice of recruiting new parents who are different from traditional adopters of relinquished infants, and they provide useful tips on how the recruitment, matching and support service can be improved.

Simmonds (2001) concluded that while 93 per cent of inquiries received by the central helpline in British Agencies for Adoption and Fostering's National Adoption Week in 1999 came from women, campaigns should be developed which highlighted the importance of fathers in the lives of adopted children. In the time that elapses between potential adoptive parents approaching an agency and the time that a child is placed, many of the would-be adopters drop out. Thoburn and colleagues (1986) found that only 8 of the 521 applicants who approached the agency had a child placed with them at the end of the study, and 5 were approved and waiting for a child to be matched with them. This makes it particularly important to scrutinise the research to see if it can lead to more reliable targeting of the sorts of parents who are likely to be successful.

The high dropout rates were also noted by Simmonds (2001), in his evaluation of the 1999 National Adoption Week. He comments:

> It is difficult to know the extent to which this should be a matter for concern. Adoption is complex and in reality something that cannot be done on the basis of either a brief acquaintance or an emotional tug at the heartstrings from a media campaign. (Simmonds, 2001, p15)

He goes on to say that the evaluation suggests that more needs to be done to provide people with the right information relevant to their circumstances. In too many cases people 'had to work hard to get any information at all and a positive or encouraging response from somebody who was interested in them'.

One point drawn out by several researchers during interviews is that an empowerment or participatory model of social work practice appears to be associated with higher rates of satisfaction among foster or adoptive parents. The way in which applicants are greeted when they first make contact with the agency is remembered by many of those interviewed by researchers, and appears to have an important impact in setting the tone for future contacts. It is clear that a less than warm initial response to a phone call, or in the course of an initial interview, may well serve to discourage some potentially successful adoptive or foster carers. Those who are finally approved describe how they had to be determined and persistent and some have commented that they fear that some potentially good applicants may not survive what they see as an obstacle course designed to put them off.

In order to avoid disappointing and spending unnecessary time with families with whom a child is unlikely to be placed, those recruiting new parents need to have a good idea of the sorts of children for whom they are likely to need placements within the next 12 months or so. An audit of children needing placement, together with a 'job description' based on research and practice experience of those likely to be successful with the different groups needing placement, are likely to be cost-effective.

The home study and assessment process

As far as we are aware, there are no research studies that evaluate the effectiveness of different methods of home study in terms of service outcomes (recruiting more families) or child outcomes (whether applicants approved in this way were more successful in helping children). What follows is therefore based on reports made to researchers by those who have experienced the home study and assessment, and on descriptions of practice in those agencies that appear to have successful outcomes.

Most agencies combine group preparation with a home study undertaken by one or more family placement workers. The consumer studies suggest that it is important to be clear and honest with the applicants about the extent to which their performance and behaviour during the group information sessions will be taken into account as part of the assessment process. It is quite obvious to potential adopters that this is inevitably the case. Thus it is likely that they will behave in a way which they hope will lead to a child being placed with them, and several have told researchers that this is what they do (Thoburn et al, 1986).

There is an acceptance by adopters and foster carers that the home study stage has to be rigorous but that an empathetic attitude by social workers is essential. The now well-established pattern of practice at this stage of the process, pioneered in the USA and in the UK in the late 1970s by Barnardo's and Parents for Children, is commended by most of those who go on to have a child placed with them. This is a time when they form important relationships with several of the agency's staff during group meetings. Even more important is the relationship they make with the individual worker who undertakes the home study. Here it is worth remembering the importance of empathy, warmth and genuineness on the part of all social workers, and of providing accurate information. Applicants are unlikely to be willing to share some of their anxieties as well as their enthusiasms if they do not feel able to trust the person undertaking the home study. Qualitative studies show that it is particularly important that applicants are able to express any reservations they may have about information given to them at this time. This may be especially important in sensitive areas such as ways of approaching the issues around the sexuality of a young person, the value of contact with members of the birth family, or questions of discipline.

Because the 'job description' for a particular family who will take a particular child is extremely varied, there is some merit in following the practice of agencies such as Parents for Children, and not completing the home study and approval until a child likely to be placed is identified. References may be taken up, and the initial part of the home study completed to the stage of the home study worker being clear that, in the right circumstances, this would be an appropriate family. It will then be possible to move through the final stages quite quickly once a child has been identified who is likely to fit in with that family. The argument for proceeding in this way is that it saves valuable time undertaking a full home study if in the end no child is placed. It also avoids the problems noted by some researchers that once a family has been fully approved, there is a tendency to want to place a child with them even if there are doubts about whether it is the right match.

The remaining stages of the home study and matching process can then consider the special needs and difficulties of the particular child to be placed, and therefore the particular characteristics and skills that will be required of the new parents. Clearly this approach is inappropriate for those with whom infants are likely to be placed since time is of the essence with very young children, and the approach may need to be adapted in the light of the National Adoption Standards (Department of Health, 2001c). However, the clear message from research on the central importance of matching children needing permanent new families with families who are likely to meet their identified needs must not be missed. To achieve this, as large a pool as possible of adopters and of long-term or permanent foster carers is needed. This points to the value of inter-agency schemes to share long-term foster families alongside established schemes to share adopters.

The amount of literature on research is very small compared to that on practice, and much more evaluation is needed of the different components that make up the home study, approval and matching stages. In this area of practice, unproven 'certainties' abound, and more work is urgently needed to seek out models of practice that are identified with positive outcome results for services and for children. It may then be possible to reduce costs in some areas, generate resources for neglected areas and ensure better outcomes for children.

Training

As with assessment, there is little evaluative research on training for adoptive parents, and all that is available are consumer comments about satisfaction or lack of it. Once more, this section has to be based on the practice of those agencies that have been evaluated, and on the views of applicants and social workers interviewed by researchers. Most agencies provide 'evaluation sheets' which are available to researchers but these tend to be far more bland than the comments made later to researchers. Generally, adoptive parents and foster carers speak highly of training, and especially of contributions from parents who have adopted or fostered children with special needs similar to those that prospective new parents are considering.

The training of new parents starts before they have been approved so that they can have the information on which to base a decision about whether they wish to continue through the home study process. It then continues after they have been approved and before the child is placed and on into the placement. However, the focus at the different stages is different. Prior to approval and before the child is matched with them, prospective new parents are given information about the agency and how it works, the legal process, the alternative legal routes to securing a permanent placement, and the different ways in which children who have special needs and emotional or behavioural difficulties might be helped with their problems. Perhaps most importantly, an aim of training is to help prospective adopters or foster carers to learn more about themselves, and begin to think more deeply about the reasons why they are considering taking a child with special needs as a member of their family.

Workers running preparation groups and undertaking home studies need themselves to be very clear about the research on the psychology of adoption, and the additional challenges and rewards of adoptive family life. In one small study, Pizey (1994) found almost total ignorance among newly approved adopters and those who had undertaken the home studies of this essential body of knowledge. Unless the workers themselves understand, for example, why identity issues will be so important to the child, they will be unable to explain to the potential adopters or foster carers why it is so important that they meet the child's birth parents, and to help them to come to an agreement with the birth parents about the part they may be able to play in the child's life as she or he grows up. Empathy exercises, which help the applicant to try more fully to understand how a parent might abuse or fail to protect a child from harm, are an important aspect of this early training. Videos can be particularly useful practice tools as they bring the views of birth family members, adopted adults and new parents into the living-rooms of potential adopters.

Early training and the home study and matching stage are interlinked. Perhaps the most important knowledge of all, which has to be explained and discussed with those who offer a long-term home for a child who may have been harmed by earlier experiences, is the child development research about the likelihood of early harm being reversible. One question that new parents should consider is what they will do if, as is unlikely but possible, a close and loving relationship does not develop between them and the child. Applicants who are not willing to face this possibility, and brush this question aside with the response that 'love will conquer all', should raise serious doubts in the minds of the social worker and panel. Information from research about the outcomes of foster or adoptive placements for the sorts of children being considered by adopters should be part of the training process – not in order to put them off but to ensure that right from the start the importance of post-placement support is built into their thinking.

There are few accounts in the research literature of the impact of training after the child has been placed, and this does not appear to have been given much space in retrospective research studies that seek adopters' opinions of the different aspects of the work. With the increased emphasis on after-adoption support there is an interest in the use of cognitive-behavioural and other approaches to helping foster carers and adoptive parents to become more skilled when children have emotional and behavioural difficulties. These approaches have been found to have some success with those parenting their own children, but Pithouse and colleagues (2002) found no evidence from their own 'semi-experimental' investigation, or a review of the literature, that they resulted in a more appropriate carer–child response from foster carers. We are not aware of any robust research studies evaluating specific training approaches with adopters or long-term foster carers, although there are descriptive accounts in the practice literature.

Preparing carers, birth families and children for placement

Work with the carers

'When they place a child they need to tell you more about the child's situation, about what has happened. They say, "they have been through a lot", but they don't say what. It would help to know so you could be lenient or take it into consideration.'
FOSTER MOTHER

'She said quite clearly over a period of time that she wanted to talk about her mum and dad. But this never happened. We had her social worker from the local authority until the adoption order but, unfortunately, she became ill. After that I had an unsatisfactory experience with the local authority workers and we also experienced more changes with the adoption agency.'
ADOPTIVE PARENT

CASE STUDY 8

Seeing the whole person: child appreciation days

Adoption services and prospective adopters often have only partial information about children waiting to be placed for adoption or long-term fostering. Barnardo's Jigsaw Service in East London has built on the model of a 'child appreciation day' to gather scattered information. The aim of the day is to bring a child to life in the mind of the prospective adopters or long-term foster carers – and to identify events and patterns that help to explain the child's history and current needs and to highlight issues that may require additional resources or training for the carers.

Significant figures in the child's life, including people who might not attend a conventional planning meeting, are invited to attend and bring with them records, photographs and mementoes. People invited could include: current and previous social workers, prospective fosterers or adopters and perhaps teachers, neighbours, childminders, and sometimes members of the child's birth family or, very rarely, the child themselves. Mementoes are collected together and given to the child after the day has finished and can be a particularly valuable outcome of the day as often these items, for example photographs, baby teeth, plaster casts, may be lost to a child who has been looked after or had multiple placements.

The information gathered during the day can also correct inaccuracies or misinformation in a child's official records, and allows people to stop and consider how the child might have been feeling, often leading to greater understanding of a child's strengths, difficulties and behaviour, and the origins of these.

Work with the birth parents

Birth parents of children adopted from care receive a generally poor service both prior to placement and during the court process (Lindley, 1994; Millham et al, 1989; Freeman and Hunt, 1998). They have also been neglected by researchers and are rarely interviewed by researchers looking at children in placement. However, as more adoption support services are set up to work with birth parents as well as adopted people and adopters, small-scale studies are beginning to appear. The permanent placement studies of Logan (1999), Neil (2000a; 2003), and Schofield and colleagues (2000) all included interviews with birth parents.

As discussed in Chapter 1 of this book, some research has been done on families with serious problems that may lead to their children needing to be looked after away from home. Once the decision has been taken that the child will not be returning home, it may be appropriate for another support worker to be allocated to the parents, or alternatively for a different worker to work with the child, although some workers are able to continue to work with the child and the two sets of parents. At this point the parents are likely to want help in working out what sort of role they can play in their child's future, including whether face-to-face or some other form of contact will be appropriate. Although unnecessary delay is to be avoided, it is essential for birth parents to have time to take stock after the court has made the decision that their child will not return to live with them.

Some authorities and children's guardians encourage courts to combine hearings on contact and freeing for adoption and hold them very shortly after the care order has been made. (This system was altered in 2002, as mentioned below.) This means that birth parents can be seriously disadvantaged at what is an emotionally difficult time. A decision has been taken about the type of permanent placement – foster care, residence order or adoption – and the type of contact to be arranged. But this has been done before it has been possible to consult parents about their wishes, after they have lost the fight to get their child back, and before services can be offered to help them to consider whether they can still play a role in the child's life as he or she moves on to become part of the new family. Research with birth parents confirms that those who are still fighting for the discharge of the order are not able to think clearly about what they will do if they lose that particular fight (see, for example, Millham et al, 1986; 1989).

The Adoption and Children Act 2002 replaced 'freeing' for adoption with placement orders, and an application for a placement order can be made at the same time as the care order. Nevertheless, it is unlikely that joint hearings would be recommended for most cases, although in a minority of cases, perhaps where the child is very young and the birth parents have already a proven record of neglect and abuse of other children, then hearings at the same time would reduce delay.

Recent developments in child placement, including the building into most placements of some form of contact – even only the exchange of letters, mean that the more traditional work of 'grief counselling' is less needed for birth parents at this stage, although it may be appropriate at a later stage. The role of the worker with the

97

birth parent is more likely to be that of helping him or her to negotiate with the temporary carers about an appropriate pattern of visiting, and then to repeat this with the new parents. They also need help in making their wishes and feelings about the nature of the substitute placement clear to those who will be making the decision.

Only a minority of studies have examined the role of adoption panels. Thoburn and colleagues (1986) interviewed panel members, and a major study by Lowe and colleagues (1999) of the adoption process added to an earlier study (Murch et al, 1993). Few permanent-placement or adoption panels appear to have fully implemented the requirement to give due consideration to the wishes and feelings of the birth parents when making a decision about whether a child should be adopted or placed in some other form of permanent placement, and about which legal route will be used to secure the placement. It seems anomalous that birth parents and older children do not attend adoption panels when their attendance at other important meetings, such as child protection conferences and reviews of looked-after children, has been well researched and found to be of value to the processes and decisions taken at these meetings (Grimshaw and Sinclair, 1997).

There are indications that with the introduction of the National Adoption Standards (Department of Health, 2001c) this is beginning to change. This is an issue discussed by Pepys and Dix (2000), while Lord and colleagues (2000) have written a legal, procedural and practice guide to panels. The general shortcomings of the panel system have been reviewed by Hanvey (2002), a former panel chairperson. He suggests that research and literature on panels over two decades suggests that the main preoccupation has been to 'tinker with procedures'.

Working with children before placement
The work undertaken with children to help them to make sense of what has happened to them and why a decision has been taken that they cannot continue to live at home has been well documented in the practice literature. However, there has been little research intended to evaluate discrete pieces of work with children, such as life-story work. Although such research may be difficult, the evident importance of identity reinforces the importance of life work and other ways of helping the child to think through the implications of the move into placement. Since a substantial minority of children placed for adoption or with long-term foster families is accommodated rather than on care orders, it is important to find ways of ensuring a 'sense of permanence' for a child and new carers during the period when the birth parent

retains parental responsibility. Suggestions as to how this might be done, drawn from research interviews, are to be found in Thoburn (1991).

Contact between the birth family and possible previous carers and the child is particularly important at this stage. While there are many ways of remaining in touch, the essence of successful contact is a clear purpose, flexibility and the opportunity to review (Argent, 2002).

Researchers interviewing birth parents (Millham et al, 1986; Lindley, 1994) conclude that it is particularly unhelpful to follow the common pattern of making contact arrangements that are both supervised and assessed, with the likelihood that an account of what happens during contact will be reported to the court. The workers in specialist contact units such as Coram Family's Meeting Place in London argue strongly that even though contact may need to be supervised in order to protect the child from possibly harmful interactions with the parents, the purpose of the worker should be to make contact as rewarding an experience as it can be for parents and children (Hinings, 1996). It should, therefore, not normally be assessed, and indeed there should be an element of 'privilege', with the parents being clear that the detail of what happens will not be fed back to the court. It is impossible for parents and children to relax and enjoy seeing each other if they know that their every move is written down. Contact for purposes of assessment by the children's guardian or by other professionals can be arranged separately from contact for purposes of mutual enjoyment, or, if relationships are more neutral or ambivalent, for keeping alive links. Neil (forthcoming) provided detailed comments from birth parents of young children and their adopters about the contact arrangements that work best.

The needs and wishes of the children should be carefully worked out and recorded before a new family is identified. From this work a profile or 'job description' of the new family being sought can be drawn up to include their culture and religion, their particular skills, whether they are experienced parents or have children in the household, along with information on their attitudes and values. Their views about the child's race, religion and culture, the sort of maltreatment the child may have experienced, the value of contact with members of the first family or previous carers, and their ability to empathise with this particular child and birth family will be especially important. It is much easier to teach new skills than to change long-established attitudes and values.

Matching the child with the family

No family should be approved if they do not have the ability, or the potential to learn, to provide high-quality parenting to children who have experienced trauma and disruptions in their early lives. The art of making permanent placements appears to be in learning what the new parents have to give and what they will expect in return, and matching these with what the child needs and is willing to take from new parents, and also what the child can give back to them. Child development research offers assistance in compiling a profile of how a particular child might react to placement with a new family.

CASE STUDY 9

Extending the role of adoption panels

At the Midlands New Families service (MNF), adoption panels do not stop at the approval of adopters but also view linking material that matches the child under consideration for placement with the approved carer, and examines the quality of the information about the child provided to the prospective adopter(s). (The local authority panel nevertheless makes the recommendation on linking.) The local authority social worker is asked to attend the panel meeting to highlight and address any gaps in the child's history. The panel looks at the supporting information about the child and requests further information where appropriate, negotiating with the local authority to provide further support services such as psychological assessment or treatment in support of the placement.

Formal evaluation of the success of this approach would require a longitudinal comparative study of the rate of disruption. However, the service manager finds the process useful in securing resources at the start of a placement where a child has particular needs, and in providing fuller information to prospective adopters. While the local authority is under no obligation to act on the panel's request for further resources or support, the service finds that in practice their requests are met.

Families have had particular difficulty in caring for children who have been sexually abused, or with serious behaviour problems, when the families have not been informed about this in advance (Barth, 1988). Families who adopted children considerably different from the kind they had hoped for had more difficult placements. Barth also found, however, that such problems could be lessened by providing families with more information about the child before adoption. These findings suggest that the practice of 'stretching', which involves accepting children who are different from those anticipated as a result of not being told of these differences, is a serious threat to securing a positive adoption.

It is desirable that the worker who has come to know the family well in the process of undertaking the home study has a major role to play in the matching process. If anything other than very indirect contact with birth parents is likely to be part of the placement plan, Ryburn (1994a) and Fratter (1996) suggest that contact plans will be facilitated if the birth parents and the new parents meet to discuss what each of them considers appropriate arrangements. Thoburn and colleagues (1986) noted the delicacy of this stage and the importance of good working relationships between the workers for the three parties.

> 'I was very sympathetic to her parents. I tried to understand that this was a young Asian mother new to this country, who was very unsupported and that perhaps her husband hadn't been that responsible in his attitude toward keeping the family together. There had been some problem with him because he had been unemployed, so there were a lot of issues. So I had a lot of sympathy with her mother from the start. I liked her enormously. I was just so sad for her. She was so isolated and did not have the capacity to be a parent. I remember thanking her for giving us two children, you know, her loss was our gain, and this feeling stayed with me for a long time. I do not see her as a threat. If the children wanted to search for her, I would support them. She is part of their identity, and it is their choice.'
> ASIAN ADOPTIVE MOTHER

Researchers who interviewed children's social workers and link workers for the new families (Macaskill, 1985b; Reich and Lewis, 1986; Thoburn et al, 1986) note their strong feelings of empathy for the families they have come to know through the home study. It is important that they have time to discuss their feelings about whether a potential placement is an appropriate match for the child and family, and how the introductions and further negotiations should take place. Several studies report cases where one or other worker had uncertainties at this stage, but which they did not bring into the open. Recriminations then followed between workers when there were later problems.

Introductions and making the move

The introduction of the new family and the child to each other is another delicate stage of the process, and families interviewed by researchers had much to say on this subject. The social workers interviewed by Thoburn and colleagues (1986) spoke of the importance of careful stage management and planning by the child's worker and the family's worker. There is support in the research for the view that, since the emphasis in future will be on the crucial role of the new family, it is the support worker for the family who must be in the driving-seat at this stage and throughout the introductory process, but keeping in close touch with the child's worker.

Although in the past it has been customary to end contact with the birth parents before the introductions begin 'to allow the child to settle' and to allow the new parents space to 'claim' the child, there appears to be no support for this in the research, or indeed in child development theory. If comfortable contact between the child and birth parents, brothers and sisters or other relatives has been established with the child in a temporary placement, the research on separation and loss suggests that it will be inappropriate to associate what is meant to be a pleasurable experience for the child, meeting and joining a new family, with the cutting off of contact with people who represent continuity with the past, and in some cases will be sorely missed.

Fitzgerald (1983) found an association between disruption of a placement and the child not being reconciled to the need to lose the first family before joining a new one. Early practice experience when making new family placements was largely developed with children who had been away from their parents for several years and who had already 'cut their losses' and wanted a new family. It was not necessary, therefore, to inflict the pain of artificially severing significant attachments since, for many of these older children, links had already withered (Millham et al, 1986).

Attachment theory and research clearly indicate that the loss of adults to whom the child is attached, whether fully, ambivalently or anxiously, will be distressing. In some cases it will have a long-term significantly harmful impact. Continued contact with parents, relatives or siblings may mean that this additional harm can be avoided, and can provide continuity when new attachments are being formed. This applies to foster carers or residential workers to whom the child has become attached as well as to members of the birth family. The views of young people who spoke to Joan Fratter (1996) about their experience of continued contact after placement support this interpretation of child development research.

Support after placement

Research evidence and practitioners agree that, once a child has been placed, it will be appropriate in the majority of cases for the long-term support of the placement to be undertaken by the specialist who did the home study and approval work. At the time of placement, the person who is most likely to help the parents and children in the new family to develop a sense of commitment and permanence is the worker in whom the new parents already have confidence. Many adopters or long-term foster carers have told researchers about their nervousness when visited by the child's worker.

Children also report being made anxious by a visit from the worker who has been responsible for moving them around in the past. Thus, the child's worker is best seen as a caring presence in the background who arrives at the time when the placement is reviewed, but otherwise leaves the support to the new family's worker or undertakes an agreed piece of work at the request of child, new family, or the support worker. There will, of course, be good reasons in some cases for the child's worker to be the main support worker, and new parents and children should have a say in how the respective roles are worked out.

'Post-adoption support has been a very good idea. It's nice to have the child with you [at a celebration of adoption day] and it's nice to meet up, share thoughts, ideas and moans and groans. There can be behavioural problems, attachment problems, it's nice to know you can pick up the phone.'
ADOPTIVE PARENT

'Be assertive with social workers – make sure you know your rights for help. Respite, particularly, insist on respite. If your relationship doesn't hold together, the kids have had it. Make sure you get practical help. I don't see why foster parents should have it and not adopters, and make sure that children who have been harmed get psychotherapy. Get the service for them.'
ADOPTIVE PARENT

'Yes, in a lot of ways there were some things you could say, yes, this comes from a black social worker. Talking to her I felt free to say just how I felt about it. But if I was dealing with a white social worker, I would probably be wondering: "Now, how do I put this so it doesn't seem as if I'm trying to make trouble, but they do understand what I am saying?" It's not essential to have [a black social worker] but it's necessary that it should be made available. I think that's the right way to put it. A black carer could find it quite easy to get on with a

white worker without any qualms. But if that is requested – a black worker – they should try to meet that.'
FOSTER CARER

'Social workers just sit there and don't think of saying that you must get on quickly to psychotherapists to get the help you need. They were thinking of getting us in for family therapy, but that was very threatening. We didn't want that.'
ADOPTIVE PARENT

CASE STUDY 10

Sharing care for children adopted by single people

A joint residency agreement for two children each adopted by a single person who shared a house formed a safety net for the adoptive parents, who knew that if anything happened to one of them neither child would go back into residential care. They and another adoptive family were approved and trained to provide each other with short-break care.

What young people joining long-term or adoptive families say most emphatically and most clearly is that they want to be allowed to settle in and be 'a normal member of the family'. Any therapy deemed necessary at these early stages has to be carefully negotiated with the young person. However, several studies report positive feedback from young people and their adoptive parents about the help provided by educational and clinical psychologists. Another strong message from most studies is that, although a small proportion would prefer not to, most would like to see such professionals more frequently than they do.

Studies which have followed placements for several years after the child joined the new family have found that therapeutic intervention in the early years when the child is settling in is not usually appropriate (Argent, 1988; Macaskill, 1985b; Reich and Lewis, 1986; Thoburn et al, 1986; Thoburn, 1990; Yates, 1985). At that stage, general supportive casework to the new family as a whole will often include the continuation of the life-story work that may be undertaken jointly by the new family's support worker and the new parents. In the longer term, however, perhaps in the third, fourth or fifth years after placement when the new family is established as a family, therapy may become necessary with those children who have suffered abuse, neglect or other serious adversity.

The source of this therapeutic intervention needs to be discussed carefully with family members. In some cases they prefer their own support worker to offer the service, perhaps jointly with a psychologist or therapist from a specialist unit. Others, however, prefer to go to an agency specialising in post-adoption work, such as one of the post-adoption centres now established in different parts of the country. If therapeutic intervention is needed, careful thought must be given to whether it should be offered to the child alone, or jointly with the adopters or foster carers. Again the principles of family support work outlined in Chapter 1 should be observed, with the family members being asked about the approach they would find most helpful. Post-adoption workers and researchers (Howe and Hinings, 1989a) report that adoptive families find it particularly irritating to be told that the way their family functions is the problem, when they had previously functioned very adequately as a family until they encountered the stresses and strains of taking a child with very special needs.

Children who resist becoming attached to their new families have, in recent years, been the subject of much discussion, and the term 'reactive attachment disorder' has come into use. This is not a new phenomenon and many examples are to be found in the qualitative research studies. Several therapies have been tried, and new therapies based on attachment theory are being suggested, but we are not aware of evaluations of any of these.

Rushton and colleagues (1995) have described in detail the parenting styles of the adoptive and foster families of boys placed between the age of 5 and 9. They were followed up at intervals over eight years, and details were reported about their behaviour, the quality of parenting (as rated by the researchers in terms of consistency, sensitivity and understanding) and contacts with social workers. With such small numbers (only 16 at the final stage) it was difficult to disentangle the quality of parenting from the nature of the children that made them more difficult to parent. The researchers concluded that 'all three of those with high background adversity but with highly positive parenting during the first month of the placement showed good or moderate outcomes, whereas five out of six of those with less positive parenting had outcomes that were poor or disrupted' (Rushton et al, 1995, p693). This suggests that efforts to enhance the quality of parenting may pay dividends, and that parenting and attachment should not be seen as synonymous.

Howe (1996) would concur, as would several of the young people interviewed by researchers (for example, Thoburn, 1990; Fratter, 1996). Even if they never became fully attached to their new parents, some young people interviewed were appreciative of the good parenting they received and felt they had been given a better start in adult life than they would otherwise have had. In this light, the Looking After Children schedules may be helpful in ensuring that the elements of good parenting are provided. Batty (1991) and Macaskill (1991) give advice on the special parenting needs of sexually abused children but do not differentiate between short-term and intermediate and permanent carers.

Other writers, including O'Hara and Hoggan (1988) in Lothian, those in the collection on post-adoption services by Argent (1988), and Festinger (1983), Nelson (1985) and Barth (1988) in America, have written of the importance of providing: adequate financial support and insurance cover; teen-sitting services; support from adopters' groups; and provision of short-break care. Some children will be able to stay in touch with their new parents only if there are regular or even long-term breaks, as with the provision of boarding education (Nelson, 1985).

Turning to work with the birth family, both the Children Act and adoption legislation and standards require that a service should be available to help them with problems arising from the adoption. In the early stages the sort of help that may be needed will include negotiating an appropriate pattern of direct or indirect contact. Birth parents will want to talk through their feelings as they see their child moving emotionally towards the new parents. As with the children, it will be some time after the actual placement that the birth parents are most likely to move from needing an essentially supportive relationship (help them with negotiation and with the skills to fulfil a different role in the child's life), to one where they may wish to seek group or individual therapy.

How can research help permanent family placement?

There is a lack of fit between current concerns about the adoption process and the research evidence. Much attention is given to unnecessary delay in reaching a decision that a child should be placed, proceeding to placement and then to adoption. 'Common sense' and theories of child development suggest that delay is likely to be associated with poorer outcomes. However, no empirical study has shown this to be the case. One of the problems for researchers, policy-makers and practitioners is that there can be no single 'best practice' for permanent new family placement when the children themselves have such different needs. Average timescales are meaningless.

A delay of six months before placing a relinquished infant will take the child past the age at which risks start to accumulate. On the other hand, to expect a traumatised 9-year-old to have cut her losses on parents she still cares and worries about and move on to a new 'forever family' all within six months may compound the significant harm she has already suffered. Consumer studies provide evidence of adopters and some children greatly regretting the lost months or years before they came together as a family, but other new parents and young people, who are heard often only when the placement breaks down, say it was all done too quickly, and their opinions and doubts were not heeded.

Despite the many published studies, robust research on outcomes is only beginning to unravel the complex biographies, relationships, feelings, attitudes, practices and events that contribute to the success or otherwise of permanent family placements. Each year, more pieces of the puzzle are slotted in. We have given details here of some of the most relevant British studies and information on new research from across the world. We have not, in the space available, tackled the often very public issue of inter-country adoption, but refer the reader to the volume on research policy and practice edited by Selman (2000).

In drawing together what we do know, we conclude that, when children of any age cannot go safely home or to relatives, it is more likely than not that their needs can be met and their well-being enhanced by being placed with a permanent new family. No *group* of child is unsuitable for permanent family placement but, for a minority of *individual* children, the nature of their attachments to the parents they cannot safely live with, or the damaging impact of trauma, separation and loss, will make the risks to themselves and to any available new family too high. Other older children will just decline the offer and prefer either group living, or a move to independence – or to remain in 'temporary' care.

Once the decision to look for a new family has been taken, a careful assessment and scrutiny of the research will take the worker some way towards deciding what sort of placement and what sort of practice will be more likely to succeed with that particular child. Guidance can be helpful, but rigid rules based on age or type of maltreatment are best avoided. For some children, only adoption, and for others, only foster placement will be acceptable. For some, legal status is much less important than finding a family that can empathise with the child's earlier life and facilitate the appropriate form of contact with birth parents and siblings. In such circumstances, the outcome research would support a twin-track approach of looking, as soon as it becomes clear that the child cannot go safely home, for either an adoptive or a foster family, who can meet the child's needs, thus widening the pool of potential families.

Finally, the members of new families have post-placement needs of their own. They tend to make fewer requests for help in their own right than do adopted adults and birth parents. However, several researchers have pointed out that adopters, long-term foster carers and birth children and relatives can suffer emotional harm as a consequence of a difficult placement, whether it lasts or disrupts. Howe and Hinings (1989) looked at the work of the Post-Adoption Centre in London. Thoburn (1990) interviewed foster carers and adopted parents whose children are adults, as did Howe (1996). Berridge and Cleaver (1987) interviewed long-term foster carers who experienced a placement breakdown. All of these give accounts of the distress of those who have given so much of themselves and then retired hurt. Some have high enough self-esteem, especially if they have successfully parented grown-up children, to keep in touch in case the young people need them in the future (as they usually do) but others receive a devastating blow to their sense of self-worth.

Key messages emerging from research into permanent placements

- Long-term placement with relatives or friends ('kinship care'), and short-term placements that become permanent, have been found to be more successful for the full range of children than placement with families not previously known to the child ('stranger care').
- Around 5 per cent of the placements of infants made at the request of the birth parent will break down.
- Of all adopters and adults who were adopted, 80 per cent express satisfaction with their relationship.
- Successful adoptive parenting of children placed as infants relies on: the parents' ability to accept the child's dual identity; the emotional significance which the birth family will always have for the child; and the adoptive parents' view of themselves as new parents.
- For older children, age at placement is key. Beyond the age of 6 months,

vulnerability to emotional problems stemming from difficulties with attachment, separation and loss increase with age at placement.

- On average, one in five placements from care with adoptive parents or permanent foster carers not previously known to the child breaks down within five years of placement. However, this figure may not be helpful as so much depends on the age of the child and other characteristics at the time of placement.

- Children who have been institutionalised, who have behavioural or other emotional difficulties, or who have been abused or neglected face a greater likelihood of their placement breaking down.

- Being placed with siblings has been found by some researchers to be associated with more successful outcome. Continued contact with birth parents, relatives or siblings, and past foster carers can provide continuity for children in forming attachments to new families.

- Having continued contact with members of the birth family is also found in some studies to be associated with a reduced risk of breakdown but appears to make no difference in others.

- Some studies have found that children who have physical or learning disabilities generally do as well or better when placed with new parents than children who are in other respects similar.

- When age at placement and other variables are held constant, there are no differences in breakdown rates between adoptive placements and placements with permanent foster families. Qualitative studies find that some children prefer to be fostered and others prefer to be adopted.

- Some studies have shown that children of mixed racial heritage are more likely to experience placement breakdown than either black or white children.

- Many studies of the placement of infants and of older children have found that placement breakdown was associated with the existence of a birth child close in age to the child being placed.

- It is important for new parents to feel comfortable about integrating a child's early history into their family life.

- Single people and couples of many different types have successfully adopted or permanently fostered children who have experienced difficulties in their early lives or are disabled.

- Providing information to new parents in advance of placement about sexual abuse and behaviour problems can help to lessen the problems that may arise for new families.

4 Social and policy developments and a new research agenda

A review of the existing body of research provides many useful lessons for policy and practice in the field of family placement. However, there are still many gaps in our knowledge, and further research is required to address the questions emerging in a changing practice environment. Policy and practice developments have, for example, meant that many more children continue to be placed with new parents while also maintaining some continued contact with a birth parent or other relative.

Much practice now involves 'grief work' with the child and the birth parents but if there is some continued contact the nature of this work will change. How children are told about their origins will be different if the parent reappears from time to time, or writes letters. And searching by adopted people will gradually become a less significant part of post-adoption work since, if you don't lose contact, you don't have to search. In its place comes the work of facilitating a wide range of contact arrangements and helping children as they grow up to make their own decisions about meeting their birth families.

The placement of children of minority ethnic origin who are looked after by local authorities is changing, as more are placed with new parents of the same ethnic background. The research agenda should change accordingly, from investigations of transracial placements to those of children in the care of families of a similar cultural heritage. On the other hand, a new generation of children placed from overseas with racially and culturally different families will be growing to maturity. Many of them will have experienced extreme material and psychological deprivation rather than the parental maltreatment experienced by those placed from care. Data must be collected now so that we can learn from what happens to these children as they grow up and when they move into adult life.

Many adoptive and permanent foster families will have had different experiences from those who adopted or fostered in the past. The sadness and stress of infertility affects increasing numbers of people who wish to experience parenthood but only a small percentage of them will have a baby placed with them for adoption, although this may be balanced by increasing numbers adopting from overseas. More choices, with a growing number of assisted reproduction procedures and surrogacy, will have lengthened the time and increased the stress on individuals and marriages before the decision is taken to apply to adopt. Adopters will almost certainly be older, on average, than those included in past research studies. A study of social trends suggests that more of the marriages of adoptive parents will break up after the placement. More placements will be made with parents who have had a previous marriage and have children who are still dependent, as well as with single people and with same-sex partnerships.

These and many other changes make it essential that longitudinal studies start now. We can continue to fill the many gaps in our knowledge of what works in temporary and permanent family placement practice, but can also check whether existing knowledge about what works is still relevant. Alongside these longitudinal studies, which must be large enough to include significant numbers of children who experience a range of out-of-home placements, smaller cohort studies are needed of children with similar problems or special needs. These might include, for example, infants whose parents have a learning disability or a mental illness, or toddlers who are well attached to a parent who marries or sets up home with a man with convictions for sexual abuse of older children. Some of those in these studies will remain at home and perhaps receive short-break care services and others will be placed with new parents or with relatives. Such studies should build in specific outcome measures, and should carefully describe the different methods used at the different stages of the placement process, so that we can add a few more pieces to the 'what works' jigsaw.

Meanwhile, many of the problems, as well as the satisfactions and successes, of family placement remain with us even as we experience and foresee these changes. Another constant is the right of children and families to expect that practitioners, managers and agencies act not merely with good intentions but also on the basis of sound knowledge. Our hope is that this book has provided a framework, and even filled in a few areas of detail, to allow practitioners, managers and agencies to seek that goal.

References

Aldgate, J (1980) Identification of factors which influence length of stay in care. In Triseliotis, JP (ed) *New developments in foster care and adoption*. Routledge, London.

Aldgate, J (1990) Foster children at school: success or failure? *Adoption and Fostering* 14(4): 38–49.

Aldgate, J (1993) Respite care for children: an old remedy in a new package. In Marsh, P, Triseliotis, J (eds) *Prevention and reunification in child care*. Batsford, London.

Aldgate, J, Bradley, M (1999), *Supporting families through short-term fostering*. The Stationery Office, London.

Aldgate, J, Hawley, D (1986a) *Recollections of disruption*. NFCA, London.

Aldgate, J, Hawley, D (1986b) Helping foster families through disruption. *Adoption and Fostering* 10(2): 44–49.

Aldgate, J, Colton, M, Ghate, D, Heath, A (1992) Educational attainment and stability in long-term foster care. *Children and Society* 2(6): 91–103.

Aldgate, J, Pratt, R, Duggan, M (1989) Using care away from home to prevent family breakdown. *Adoption and Fostering* 13(2):32-37.

Almas, T (1991) *Fostering and adoption in Asian families*. Barnardo's, Yorkshire.

Altstein, H, Simon, R (1991) *Intercountry adoption: a multinational perspective*. Praeger, New York.

Ames, J (1993) *We have learned a lot from them: foster care for young people with learning disabilities*. Barnardo's/ National Children's Bureau, Barkingside.

Argent, H (1984) *Find me a family*. Souvenir Press, London.

Argent, H (ed) (1988) *Keeping the doors open*. London: British Agencies for Adoption and Fostering.

Argent, H (1998) *Whatever happened to Adam? Stories of disabled people who were adopted or fostered*. British Agencies for Adoption and Fostering, London.

Argent, H (ed) (2002) *Staying connected: managing contact arrangements in adoption*. BAAF Adoption and Fostering, London.

Audit Commission (1994) *Seen but not heard*. HMSO, London.

Baddredine, K, Idstrom, U (1995) Alternative options provided for children in foster care: different forms of placement in Sweden. In Documentation of the European International Foster Care Organisations conference, *Foster children in a changing world*, Berlin.

Bailey, S, Thoburn, J, Wakeham, H (2002) Using the 'looking after children' dimensions to collect aggregate data on well-being. *Child and Family Social Work* 7(3): 189–201.

Barclay Committee (1982) *Social workers: their roles and tasks*. National Institute for Social Work/ Bedford Square Press, London.

Barn, R (1990) Black children in local authority care: admission patterns. *New Community* 16(2): 229–246.

Barn, R (1993a) *Black children in the public care system*. Batsford/ British Agencies for Adoption and Fostering, London.

Barn, R (1993b) Black and white child carers: a different reality. In Marsh, P, Triseliotis, J (eds) *Prevention and reunification in child care*. Batsford, London.

Barn, R (2001) *Black youth on the margins: a research review*. York Publishing Services/ Joseph Rowntree Foundation, York.

Barn, R, Sinclair, R, Ferdinand, D (1997) *Acting on principle: an examination of race and ethnicity in social services provision for children*. British Agencies for Adoption and Fostering, London.

Barnardo's (1995) *Guide to family placement*. Family and Young People Support Service, Barnardo's, Barkingside.

Barth, R (1988) Disruption in older child adoptions. *Public Welfare*, Winter.

Barth, R, Berry, M (1988) *Adoption and disruption: rates, risk and responses*. Aldine de Gruyter, New York.

Barth, R, Berry, M, Carson, M, Goodfield, R, Feinberg, B (1986) Contributors to disruption and dissolution of older-child adoptions. *Child Welfare* 65(4): 359-372.

Barth, R, Courtney, M, Berrick, J, Albert, V (1998) *From child abuse to permanency planning*. Aldine de Gruyter, New York.

Batty, D (ed) (1991) *Sexually abused children – making their placements work*. British Agencies for Adoption and Fostering, London.

Bayley, M (1987) *Mental handicap and community care.* Routledge and Kegan Paul, London.

Bebbington, A, Miles, J (1989) The background of children who enter local authority care. *British Journal of Social Work* (19)5: 349–368.

Bebbington, A, Miles, J (1990) The supply of foster families for children in care. *British Journal of Social Work* 20: 283–307.

Beresford, B (2002) Preventing social exclusion of disabled children. In McNeish, D, Newman, T, Roberts, H, *What works for children.* Open University Press, Buckingham.

Beresford, B, Sloper, P, Baldwin, S, Newman, T (1996) *What works in services for families with a disabled child?* Barnardo's, Barkingside.

Berridge, D (1996) *Foster care: a research review.* The Stationery Office, London.

Berridge, D (1997) *Foster care: a research review.* The Stationery Office, London.

Berridge, D, Cleaver, H (1987) *Foster home breakdown.* Basil Blackwell, Oxford.

Berridge, D, Smith, P (1993) *Ethnicity and child care placements.* National Children's Bureau, London.

Biestek, F (1961) *The casework relationship.* Allen & Unwin, London.

Bohman, M (1970) *Adopted children and their families.* Proprius, Stockholm.

Bohman, M, Sigvardsson, S (1980) Negative social heritage. *Adoption and Fostering* (101)3: 25-31.

Borland, M, O'Hara, G, Triseliotis, J (1991) Placement outcomes for children with special needs. *Adoption and Fostering* 15(2): 18–28.

Bowlby, J (1953) *Child care and the growth of love.* Penguin Books, Harmondsworth.

Broad, B, Hayes, B, Rushforth, C (2001) *Kith and kin: kinship care for vulnerable young people.* Joseph Rowntree Foundation, York /National Children's Bureau, London.

Brodzinsky, D, Schechter, D (eds) (1990) *The psychology of adoption.* Oxford University Press, Oxford.

Brown, S, Cohon, D, Wheeler, R (2002) African–American extended families and kinship care: how relevant is the foster care model for kinship care? *Children and Youth Services Review* 24(1/2), January/February: 53–77.

Bullard, E, Malos, E (1991) *Custodianship: caring for other people's children.* HMSO, London.

Bullock, R (1990) The implications of recent child care research findings for foster care. *Adoption and Fostering* 14(3): 43–45.

Bullock, R, Little, M, Millham, S (1993) *Going home: the return of children separated from their families*. Dartmouth, Aldershot.

Butler S, Charles, M (1999) The tangible and intangible rewards of fostering for carers. *Adoption and Fostering* 23(3): 48–58.

Caesar, G, Parchment, M, Berridge, D, Gordon, G (1994) *Black perspectives on services for children and young people in need and their families*. National Children's Bureau, London.

Caine, H (1992) *Unusual adopters*. Barnardo's, Barkingside.

Cambridgeshire County Council (1990) *Support foster care scheme: a practice manual*. Cambridgeshire County Council, Cambridge.

Cannan, C (1992) *Changing families, changing welfare*. Harvester Wheatsheaf, London.

Chand, A, Thoburn, J, Procter, J (2003) *Child welfare interventions for children and families of ethnic minority origin: a review of research*. UEA Centre for Research on the Child and the Family, Norwich.

Chamberlain, P (1990) Comparative evaluation of specialised foster care for seriously delinquent youths: a first step. *Community Alternatives: International Journal of Family Care* 2: 21–36.

Charles, M, Rashid, S, Thoburn, J (1992) The placement of black children with permanent new families. *Adoption and Fostering* 16(3): 13–19.

Cheetham, J, Fuller, R, McIvor, G, Petch, A (1992) *Evaluating social work effectiveness*. Open University Press, Buckingham.

Child Welfare League of America (1994) *Kinship care: a natural bridge*. Child Welfare League of America, Washington DC.

Cleaver, H (2000) *Fostering family contact*. The Stationery Office, London.

Cliffe, D, Berridge, D (1991) *Closing children's homes: an end to residential child care?* National Children's Bureau, London.

Colton, M (1988) *Dimensions of substitute child care: comparative study of foster and residential care practice*. Avebury, Aldershot.

Colton, M, Aldgate, J, Heath, A (1991) Behavioural problems among children in and out of care. *Social Work and Social Sciences Review* 2(3):177–191.

Convention of Scottish Local Authorities (2000) *Foster Care.* Convention of Scottish Local Authorities, Edinburgh.

Crowley, M (1982) *Preparation for foster care practice: a survey.* Social Work Monographs 11, University of East Anglia, Norwich.

Dance, C, Rushton, A (1999) Sibling separation and contact in permanent placement. In Mullender, A (ed) *We are family: sibling relationships in placement and beyond.* British Agencies for Adoption and Fostering, London.

Dando, I, Minty, B (1987) What makes good foster parents? *British Journal of Social Work* 17: 388–400.

Dartington Social Research Unit (1995) *Child protection: messages from research.* HMSO: London.

Davis, E, Kidd, L, Pringle, K (1987) *Child sexual abuse training programme for foster parents with teenage placements.* Barnardo's North East Division.

Department of Health and Social Security (1985) *Social work decisions in child care: recent research findings and their implications.* HMSO, London.

Department of Health (1991a) *The Children Act, 1989. Guidance and regulations volume 3: family placements.* HMSO, London.

Department of Health (1991b) *Patterns and outcomes in child placement: messages from current research and their implications.* HMSO, London.

Department of Health (1992) *Review of adoption law: report to ministers of an inter-departmental working group.* HMSO, London.

Department of Health (1993) *Adoption – the way forward.* HMSO, London.

Department of Health (1995a) *Inspection of local authority fostering services.* Social Services Inspectorate, HMSO, London.

Department of Health (1995b) *Independent fostering agencies' study.* Social Services Inspectorate, HMSO, London.

Department of Health (1995c) *The children (short-term placements) (miscellaneous amendments) regulations 1995.* LAC (95) 14. HMSO, London.

Department of Health (1995d) *Moving goalposts: a study of post-adoption contact in the North of England*. Social Services Inspectorate, HMSO, London.

Department of Health (1999) *Adoption now: messages from research*. Wiley, Chichester.

Department of Health (2000) *Adoption: a new approach*. The Stationery Office, London.

Department of Health (2001a) *Children adopted from care in England*. The Stationery Office, London.

Department of Health (2001b) *The Children Act now: messages from research*. Wiley, Chichester.

Department of Health (2001c) *National adoption standards for England*. The Stationery Office, London.

Department of Health (2002) *National statistics: looked after children in England 2000/2001, statistical bulletin*. The Stationery Office, London.

Department of Health (2003a) *National statistics: looked after children in England 2001/2002, statistical bulletin*. The Stationery Office, London.

Department of Health (2003b) *National statistics: children looked after by local authorities year ended 31 March 2002 England*. Government Statistical Office, London.

Department of Health, Social Services and Public Safety (2001) *Community statistics 1 April 2000 – 31 March 2001*. Department of Health, Social Services and Public Safety, Belfast.

Donley, K (1981) *Opening new doors: finding families for older and disabled children*. London: BAAF.

Douglas, A, Philpot, T (eds) (2002) *Adoption: changing families, changing times*. Routledge, London.

Ehrle, J, Geen, R (2002) Kin and non-kin foster care: findings from a national survey. *Children and Youth Services Review* 24(1/2, January/February): 15–35.

Fahlberg, V (1991) *A child's journey through placement*. Perspectives Press, New York.

Fanshel, D, Shinn, EB (1978) *Children in foster care – a longitudinal study*. Columbia University Press, New York.

Farmer, E, Parker, R (1991) *Trials and tribulations: returning children from care to their families*. HMSO, London.

Fein, E, Maluccio, AN, Hamilton, VJ, Ward, DE (1983) After foster care: permanency planning for children. *Child Welfare* 62(6): 485-558.

Ferguson, DM, Lynskey, M, Horwood, J (1995) The adolescent outcomes of adoption. A 16-year longitudinal study. *Journal of Child Psychology and Psychiatry* 36(4): 697-716.

Festinger, T (1983) *No one ever asked us … A postscript to foster care*. Columbia University Press, New York.

Festinger, T (1986) *Necessary risk: a study of adoptions and disrupted adoptive placements*. Child Welfare League of America, New York.

Fisher, M, Gibbs, I, Sinclair, I, Wilson, K (2000) Sharing the care: qualities sought by social workers of foster carers. *Child and Family Social Work* 5(3): 225–233.

Fisher, M, Marsh, P, Phillips, D, Sainsbury, E (1986) *In and out of care: the experience of children, parents and social workers*. Batsford, London.

Fitzgerald, J (1990) *Understanding disruption*. British Agencies for Adoption and Fostering, London.

Fletcher, B (1993) *Not just a name*. National Consumer Council, London.

Fratter, J (1991) Parties in the triangle. *Adoption and Fostering* 15(4): 91–98.

Fratter, J (1996) *Perspectives on adoption with contact: implications for policy and practice*. BAAF, London.

Fratter, J, Rowe, J, Sapsford, D, Thoburn, J (1991) *Permanent family placement: a decade of experience*. British Agencies for Adoption and Fostering, London.

Freeman, P, Hunt, J (1998) *Parental perspectives on care proceedings*. The Stationery Office, London.

Fry, E (1994) *On remand: foster care and the youth justice system*. National Foster Care Association, London.

Galloway, H, Wallace, F (2002) Managing contact in black kinship care. In Argent, H (ed) *Staying connected: managing contact arrangements in adoption*. BAAF Adoption and Fostering, London.

Gath, A (1983) Mentally retarded children in substitute and natural families. *Adoption and Fostering* 7(1): 35–40.

Gibbons, J (ed) (1992) *The Children Act 1989 and family support*. HMSO, London.

Gibbons, J, Gallagher, B, Bell, C, Gordon, D (1995) *Development after physical abuse in early childhood.* HMSO, London.

Gibbons, J, with Thorpe, S, Wilkinson, P (1990) *Family support and prevention.* HMSO, London.

Gill, O, Jackson, B (1983) *Adoption and race.* London, Batsford.

Goldstein, J, Freud, A, Solnit, A (1973) *Beyond the best interests of the child.* Free Press, New York.

Gray, G (2002) Avoiding disruption: concurrent planning. In Douglas, A, Philpot, T (eds) *Adoption: changing families, changing times.* Routledge, London.

Greeff, R (ed) (1999) *Fostering kinship: an international perspective on foster care by relatives.* Avebury, Aldershot.

Grimshaw, R, Sinclair, R (1997) *Planning to care.* National Children's Bureau, London.

Grotevant, HD, McRoy, RG (1998) *Openness in adoption.* Sage, New York.

Haimes, E, Timms, N (1985) *Adoption, identity and social policy.* Gower, Aldershot.

Hanvey, C (2002) Adoption panels: a critique from within. In Douglas, A, Philpot, T (eds) *Adoption: changing families, changing times.* Routledge, London.

Hart, GT (1986) *Entitled to care?* University of Salford, Salford.

Harwin, J, Owen, M (2003) *Making care orders work.* The Stationery Office, London

Harwin, J, Owen, M, Locke, R, Forester, D (2001) *Making care orders work: a study of care plans and their implementation.* The Stationery Office, London.

Hazel, N (1990) *Fostering teenagers.* National Foster Care Association, London.

Hazel, N, Fenyo, A (1993) *Free to be myself: the development of teenage fostering.* Human Services Associates, Minnesota.

Hill, M (1992) Fostering and adoption in Canada: are there lessons for Britain? *Adoption and Fostering* 16(4): 39–44.

Hill, M, Lambert, L, Triseliotis, J (1989) *Achieving adoption with love and money.* National Children's Bureau, London.

Hill, M, Lambert, L, Triseliotis, J, Buist, M (1992) Making judgements about parenting: the example of freeing for adoption. *British Journal of Social Work* 22(4): 373–389.

Hill, M, Nutter, R, Giltinan, D, Hudson, J, Galaway, B (1993) A comparative survey of specialist fostering in the UK and North America. *Adoption and Fostering* 17(2): 17–22.

Hinings, D (1996) Maintaining relationships between parents and children who live apart. In Howe, D (ed) *Attachment and loss in child and family social work.* Avebury, Aldershot.

Hodges, J, Tizard, B (1989) Social and family relationships of ex-institutional adolescents. *Journal of Child Psychology and Psychiatry* 30(1): 77-97.

Hoggan, P, Husain Sumpton, A, Ellis, W (2002) Contact in placements which match children's 'race', religion and culture. In Argent, H (ed) *Staying connected: managing contact arrangements in adoption.* BAAF Adoption and Fostering, London.

Hoksbergen, RAC (ed) (1986) *Adoption in worldwide perspective.* Zeitlinger, Lisse.

Hoksbergen, RAC (1991) Intercountry adoption: coming of age in Netherlands: basic issues, trends and developments. In Altstein, H, Simon, RJ (eds) *Intercountry adoption.* New York, Praeger.

Holman, B (2002) Letter, *Community Care*, 27 August – 4 September.

Howe, D (1992) Assessing adoptions in difficulty. *British Journal of Social Work* 22(1): 1-15.

Howe, D (1994) *On being a client.* Sage, London.

Howe, D (1996) *Adopters on adoption.* British Agencies for Adoption and Fostering, London.

Howe, D, Feast, J (2000) *Adoption, search and reunion: the long-term experience of adopted adults.* The Children's Society, London.

Howe, D, Hinings, D (1989) *The Post Adoption Centre: the first three years.* University of East Anglia, Norwich.

Howe, D, Sawbridge, P, Hinings, D (1992) *Half a million women.* Penguin, Harmondsworth.

Hundleby, M (1989) The pros and cons of specialisation. *Adoption and Fostering* 13(3): 22–25.

Hunter, A (1989) *Family placement: models of effective partnership.* Barnardo's Practice Paper, Barkingside.

Ince, L (1998) *Making it alone: a study of the care experiences of young black people.* British Agencies for Adoption and Fostering, London.

International Foster Care Organisation (1995) *Ninth international conference programme*, Bergen, July. IFCO.

Ivaldi, G (2000) *Surveying adoption*. BAAF Adoption and Fostering, London.

Irving, K (1996) Unwanted attention: the risks of using publicity in adoption and fostering. *Child Abuse Review* 5: 356–361.

Irving, K, Joss, J (1995) Using the media. Paper presented to the ninth conference of the International Foster Care Organisation, Bergen, July. IFCO.

Jackson, S, Thomas, N (1999) *What works in creating stability for looked after children?* Barnardo's, Barkingside.

Jenkins, S, Norman, E (1972) *Filial deprivation and foster care*. Columbia University Press, New York.

Jewett, CL (1978) *Adopting the older child*. The Harvard Common Press, Harvard.

Jones, MA (1985) *A second chance for families: five years later – follow up of a programme to prevent foster care*. Child Welfare League of America, New York.

Kahan, B (1979) *Growing up in care*. Blackwell, Oxford.

Katz, L, Spoonermore, N, Robinson, C (1994) *Concurrent planning*. Lutheran Social Services, Washington and Ohio.

Kelly, G (1995) Foster parents and long-term placements: key findings from a Northern Ireland study. *Children and Society* 9(2): 19–29.

Kerrane, A, Hunter, A, Lane, M (1980) *Adopting older and handicapped children*. Barnardo's, London.

Kirk, D (1965) *Shared fate*. Collier-Macmillan, London.

Kirton, D (2000) *'Race', ethnicity and adoption*. Open University Press, Buckingham.

Kirton, D (2001) Love and money: payment and the fostering task. *Child and Family Social Work* 6: 199–208.

Kirton, D, Feast, J, Howe, D (2000) Searching, reunion and transracial adoption. *Adoption and Fostering* 24(3):6-18.

Kirton, D, Beecham, J, Ogilvie, K (2003) *Remuneration and performance in foster care*. University of Kent at Canterbury, Canterbury.

Kosenson, M (1993) Descriptive study of foster and adoptive care services in a Scottish agency. *Community Alternative* 5(2).

Ladner, J (1977) *Mixed families*. Doubleday, New York.

Lahti, J (1982) A follow-up study of foster children in permanent placements. *Social Services Review*. University of Chicago, Chicago.

Lambert, L, Buist, M, Triseliotis, J, Hill, M (1990) Freeing children for adoption: the Scottish experience. *Adoption and Fostering* 14(1):36-41.

Lambert, L, Streather, J (1980) *Children in changing families*. Macmillan, London.

Lindley, B (1994) *On the receiving end: families' experiences of the court process in care and supervision proceedings under the Children Act 1989*. Family Rights Group, London.

Lindsay-Smith, C, Price, E (1980) *Barnardo's New Families Project – Glasgow. The first two years*. Barnardo's, Barkingside.

Logan, J (1999) Exchanging information post-adoption: views of adoptive parents and birth parents. *Adoption and Fostering* 23(3): 27–37.

Lothian Region Social Work Department (1995) *Involving birth parents in foster care training*. Lothian Social Work Department, Edinburgh.

Lord, J, Barker, S, Cullen, D (2000) *Effective panels: guidance on regulations, process and good practice in adoption and permanence panels*. British Agencies for Adoption and Fostering, London.

Lowe, K (1990) *Teenagers in foster care*. National Foster Care Association, London.

Lowe, N, Murch, M, Borkowski, M, Weaver, A, Beckford, V with Thomas, C (1999) *Supporting adoption: reframing the approach*. British Agencies for Adoption and Fostering, London.

Lowe, N, Murch, M with Bader, K, Borkowski, M, Copner, R, Isles, C, Shearman, J (2002) *The plan for the child: adoption or long-term fostering*. BAAF Adoption and Fostering, London.

Lynch, M, Roberts, J (1982) *Consequences of child abuse*. Academic Press, London.

Macaskill, C (1985a) *Against the odds: adopting mentally handicapped children*. British Agencies for Adoption and Fostering, London.

Macaskill, C (1985b) 'Post-adoption support' and 'Who should support after adoption?' *Adoption and Fostering* 9(1) and 9(2).

Macaskill, C (1991) *Adopting or fostering a sexually abused child.* Batsford/ British Agencies for Adoption and Fostering, London.

Macaskill, C (2002) *Safe conduct? Children in permanent placement and contact with their birth relatives.* Russell House Publishing, Lyme Regis.

Macdonald, G, Roberts, H (1995) *What works in the early years?* Barnardo's, Barkingside.

Maluccio, AN, Ainsworth, F, Thoburn, J (2000) *Child welfare outcome research in Australia, UK and USA.* Child Welfare League of America, Washington DC.

Maluccio, AN, Fein, E, Olmstead, KA (1986) *Permanency planning for children: concepts and methods.* Tavistock, London.

Mann, P (1984) *Children in care revisited.* Batsford, London.

Maughan, B, Pickles, A (1990) Adopted and illegitimate children growing up. In Robins, LJ, Rutter, M (eds) *Straight and deviant pathways from childhood to adulthood.* Cambridge University Press, Cambridge.

McAuley, C (1996) *Children in long-term foster care.* Avebury, Aldershot.

McCracken, S, Reilly, I (1998) The systematic family approach to foster care assessment. *Adoption and Fostering* 23(3): 16–27.

McNeish, D, Newman, T, Roberts, H (2002) *What works for children?* Open University Press, Buckingham.

McRoy, R (1991) Significance of ethnic and racial identity in inter-country adoption. *Adoption and Fostering* 15(4):53-60.

McRoy, R, Zurcher, L, Lauderdale, M, Anderson, R (1982) Self-esteem and racial identity in trans-racial and in-race adoptees. *Social Work* 27(6): 522–526.

McWhinnie, A (1967) *Adopted children: how they grow up.* Routledge, London.

Millham, S, Bullock, R, Hosie, K, Haak, M (1986) *Children lost in care: the family contacts of children in care.* Gower, Aldershot.

Millham, S, Bullock, R, Hosie, K, Little, M (1989) *Access disputes in child care.* Gower, Aldershot.

Minnis, H, Devine, C (2001) The effect of foster carer training on the emotional and behavioural functioning of looked-after children. *Adoption and Fostering* 25: 44–54.

Minnis, H, Devine, C, Pelosi, T (1999) Foster carers speak about training. *Adoption and Fostering* 23(2): 42–47.

Monck, E, Reynolds J, Wigfall, V (2003) *Permanent placement of young children: the role of concurrent planning.* BAAF Adoption and Fostering, London.

Mountney, J (1991) *Children with disabilities in foster care: a survey by the NFCA.* National Foster Care Association, London.

Mullender, A (ed) (1991) *Open adoption.* British Agencies for Adoption and Fostering, London.

Murch, M, Lowe, N, Borkowski, M, Copner, R, Griew, K (1993) *Pathways to Adoption Research Project.* Department of Health/ HMSO, London.

National Assembly for Wales (2002) *Social services statistics Wales 2000.* National Assembly for Wales, Cardiff.

National Foster Care Association (1988) *The challenge of foster care.* National Foster Care Association, London.

National Foster Care Association (1990) *'A problem shared' training pack.* National Foster Care Association, London.

National Foster Care Association (1993a) *Fostering a child who has been sexually abused.* National Foster Care Association, London.

National Foster Care Association (1993b) *Friends and relatives as carers: making it work.* National Foster Care Association, London.

National Foster Care Association (1994) *Choosing to foster: the challenge to care.* National Foster Care Association, London.

National Foster Care Association (1995) *Foster care finance.* National Foster Care Association, London.

National Foster Care Association (1999) *Code of practice on the recruitment, assessment, approval, training, management and support of foster carers.* National Foster Care Association on behalf of the UK Joint Working Party on Foster Care, London.

National Foster Care Association (2001) Recruitment campaign update. *Foster Care* 104: 3.

National Statistics Office (2001) *Regional trends 36.* The Stationery Office, London.

Nelson, KA (1985) *On the frontier of adoption: a study of special-needs adoptive families.* Child Welfare League of America, Washington DC.

Neil, E (1999) The sibling relationships of adopted children and patterns of contact after adoption. In Mullender, A (ed) *We are family: sibling relationships in placement and beyond.* British Agencies for Adoption and Fostering, London.

Neil, E (2000a) Contact with birth relatives after adoption: a study of young, recently placed children. Unpublished PhD thesis, University of East Anglia, Norwich.

Neil, E (2000b) The reasons young people are placed for adoption: findings from a recently placed sample and implications for future identity issues. *Child and Family Social Work* 5(4): 303–316.

Neil, E (2002a) Contact after adoption: the role of agencies in making and supporting adoption plans. *Adoption and Fostering* 26(1): 25–38.

Neil, E (2002b) Managing face to face contact for young adopted children. In Argent, H (ed) *Staying connected: managing contact arrangements in adoption.* BAAF Adoption and Fostering, London.

Neil, E (2003) Accepting the reality of adoption: birth relatives' experiences of face to face contact. *Adoption and Fostering* 27(2): 32-43.

Neil, E, Beek, M, Schofield, G (2003) Thinking about and managing contact in permanent placements: the differences and similarities between adoptive parents and foster carers. *Clinical Child Psychology and Psychiatry* 8(3):401-418.

Nixon, S (1997) The limits of support in foster care. *British Journal of Social Work* 27: 913–930.

Nixon, S (2000) Safe care, abuse and allegations of abuse in foster care. In Kelly, G, Gilligan, R (eds) *Issues in foster care: policy, practice and research.* Jessica Kingsley Publishers, London.

Nutter, R, Hudson, J, Galaway, B, Hill, M, Giltinan, D (1993a) Where children live before and after specialist foster care. Paper presented to the 8th International Foster Care Organisation's conference, July, Dublin.

Nutter, R, Hudson, J, Galaway, B (1993b) Treatment foster care: where it came from and where it is. Paper presented to the 70th Annual Meeting of the American Orthopsychiatric Association.

O'Hara, G (1986) Developing post placement services in Lothian. *Adoption and Fostering* 10(4): 38–42.

O'Hara, G (1991) Placing children with special needs: outcomes and implications for practice. *Adoption and Fostering* 15(4): 24–30.

O'Hara, J, Hoggan, P (1988) Permanent substitute family care in Lothian – placement outcomes. *Adoption and Fostering* 12(3):35-38.

Oswin, M (1984) *They keep going away.* King Edward's Hospital Fund for London, London.

Owen, M (1996) *Single-person adoption, report to the Department of Health.* University of Bristol, Bristol.

Packman, J, Hall, C (1998) *Care to accommodation.* The Stationery Office, London.

Packman, J with Randall, J, Jacques, N (1986) *Who needs care? Social work decisions about children.* Blackwell, Oxford.

Parker, RA, Ward, H, Jackson, S, Aldgate, J, Wedge, P (1991) *Assessing outcomes in child care.* HMSO, London.

Part, D (1993) Fostering as seen by the carers' own children. *Adoption and Fostering* 17(1): 26–31.

Pecora, PJ, Le Prohn, NC, Nollan, K (1998) *How are the children doing? Assessing your outcomes in family foster care.* The Casey Family Programme, Seattle WA.

Pepys, S, Dix, J (2000) Inviting applicants, birth parents and young people to attend adoption panels:how it works in practice. *Adoption and Fostering* 24(4): 44-49.

Performance and Innovation Unit (2000) *Review of adoption: issues for consultation.* Cabinet Office, London.

Phillips, R, McWilliam, E (eds) (1996) *Working with adoptive families.* BAAF, London.

Philpot, T (2001) *A very private practice: an investigation into private fostering.* BAAF Adoption and Fostering, London.

Philpot, T, Broad, B (2003) *Family solutions, family problems: kinship care for children in need: an agenda for change.* Children and Families Research Unit, De Montfort University, Leicester.

Pine, B, Healy, LM, Maluccio, AN (2002) Developing measurable programme objectives: a key to evaluation of family reunification programmes. In Vecchiato, T, Maluccio, AN, Canali, C. *Evaluation in child and family services.* Aldine de Gruyter, New York.

Pinkerton, J (1994) *In care at home.* Aldershot. Avebury.

Pithouse, A, Parry, O (1997) Fostering in Wales: the all Wales review. *Adoption and Fostering* 21(2): 41–49.

Pithouse, A, Hill-Tout, J, Lowe, K (2002) Training foster carers in challenging behaviour: a case study in disappointment. *Child and Family Social Work* 7(3) 203–214.

Pithouse, A, Young, C, Butler, I (1994) *The all Wales review: local authority fostering services.* University of Wales, Cardiff.

Pizey, C (1994) Issues of identity and loss in the preparation and assessment of prospective adopters of young children. *Adoption and Fostering* 18(2): 44-49.

Pugh, G (1996) Seen but not heard: addressing the needs of children who foster. *Adoption and Fostering* 20(1): 35–41.

Quinton, D, Selwyn, J (1998) Contact with birth parents in adoption – a response to Ryburn. *Child and Family Law Quarterly* 10(4): 349–361.

Quinton, D, Rushton, A, Dance, D, Mayes, D (1997) Contact between children placed away from home and their birth parents: research issues and evidence. *Clinical Child Psychology and Psychiatry* 2(3): 393–413.

Quinton, D, Rushton, A, Dance, C, Mayes, D (1998) *Joining new families: a study of adoption and fostering in middle childhood.* John Wiley & Sons, Chichester.

Raynor, L (1980) *The adopted child comes of age.* Allen and Unwin, London.

Reich, D, Lewis, J (1986) Placement by parents for children. In Wedge, P, Thoburn, J (eds) *Finding families for hard-to-place children.* BAAF, London.

Rhodes, P (1993) Charitable vocation or 'proper job'? The role of payment in foster care. *Adoption and Fostering* 17(1): 8–13.

Richards, A (2001) *Second time around.* Family Rights Group, London.

Rickford, F (2002) We're listening… *Community Care* 25 April – 1 May: 34–35.

Robinson, C (1987) Key issues for social workers placing children for family-based respite care. *British Journal of Social Work* 17(3): 25-84.

Rowe, J (1988) Relatives as foster parents. In Holman, R, *Planning for children*. Family Rights Group, London.

Rowe, J, Cain, H, Hundleby, M, Keane, A (1984) *Long-term foster care*. Batsford, London.

Rowe, J, Hundleby, M, Garnett, L (1989) *Child care now – a survey of placement patterns*. British Agencies for Adoption and Fostering, London.

Rushton, A, Minnis, H (1997) Annotation: transracial family placements. *Journal of Child Development and Psychology* 28(2): 157–159.

Rushton, A, Treseder, J (1986) Developmental recovery. *Adoption and Fostering* 10(3): 54-56.

Rushton, A, Treseder, J, Quinton, D (1988) *New parents for older children*. British Agencies for Adoption and Fostering, London.

Rushton, A, Treseder, J, Quinton, D (1993) New parents for older children: support services during eight years of placement. *Adoption and Fostering* 17: 39–45.

Rushton, A, Treseder, J, Quinton, D (1995) An eight-year prospective study of older boys placed in permanent substitute families. *Journal of Child Psychology and Psychiatry* 36(4): 687-696.

Rushton, A, Dance, C, Quinton, D, Mayes, D (2001) *Siblings in late permanent placement*. BAAF Adoption and Fostering, London.

Russell, C (1995) Parenting the second time around: grandparents as carers in child protection cases. MA dissertation. University of East Anglia, Norwich.

Rutter, M, The English and Romanian Adoptees Study Group (1998) Development catch-up, and deficit, following adoption after severe global early privation. *Journal of Child Psychology and Psychiatry* 39: 465–476.

Rutter, M, Quinton, D, Liddle, C (1983) Parenting in two generations: looking backwards and looking forwards. In Madge, N (ed) *Families at risk*. Heinemann, London.

Ryburn, M (1991) The myth of assessment. *Adoption and Fostering* 15(1): 76–80.

Ryburn, M (1994a) *Open adoption: research, theory and practice*. Avebury, Aldershot.

Ryburn, M (ed) (1994b) *Contested adoptions: research, law, policy and practice*. Arena, Aldershot.

Ryburn, M (1997) In whose best interests? Post-adoption contact with the birth family. *Child and Family Law Quarterly* 10(4): 53.

Sachdev, P (1989) The triangle of fear: fallacies and facts. *Child Welfare* LXVIII(5): 491–503.

Sapsford, D (1991) Appendix in Fratter, J, Rowe, J, Sapsford, D, Thoburn, J, *Permanent family placement: a decade of experience*. British Agencies for Adoption and Fostering, London.

Sawbridge, P (1983) *Parents for children. Twelve practice papers*. British Agencies for Adoption and Fostering, London.

Schofield, G (2003) *Part of the family: pathways through foster care*. BAAF Adoption and Fostering, London.

Schofield, G, Beek, M, Sargent, K, with Thoburn, J (2000) *Growing up in foster care*. British Agencies for Adoption and Fostering, London.

Scottish Executive (2002) *Looked after children in the year to 31 March 2001*. Scottish Executive, Edinburgh.

Sellick, C (1992) *Supporting short-term foster carers*. Avebury, Aldershot.

Sellick, C (1996) Short-term foster care. In Hill, M, Aldgate, J (eds) *Child welfare services: developments in law, policy, practice and research*. Jessica Kingsley Publishers, London.

Sellick, C (1999a). Independent fostering agencies: providing high quality services to children and carers? *Adoption and Fostering* 24(1): 7–14.

Sellick, C (1999b) The role of social workers in supporting and developing the work of foster carers. In Hill, M (ed) *Signposts in fostering: policy, practice and research issues*. British Agencies for Adoption and Fostering, London.

Sellick, C (2002) The aims and principles of independent fostering agencies: a view from the inside. *Adoption and Fostering* 26(1): 56–63.

Sellick, C, Connolly, J (2001) *National survey of independent fostering agencies*. Centre for Research on the Child and the Family, University of East Anglia, Norwich.

Sellick, C, Connolly, J (2002) Independent fostering agencies uncovered: the findings of a national study. *Child and Family Social Work* 7(2): 107–120.

Sellick, C, Thoburn, J (1996) *What works in family placement?* Barnardo's, Barkingside.

Selman, P (ed) (2000) *Intercountry adoption: developments, trends and perspectives.* British Agencies for Adoption and Fostering, London.

Selman, P, Wells, S (1996) Post-adoption issues in inter-country adoption. In Phillips, R, McWilliams, E (eds) *After adoption.* British Agencies for Adoption and Fostering, London.

Selwyn, J, Sturgess, W, Quinton, D, Baxter, K (forthcoming) *Costs and outcomes for non-infant adoptions.* School for Policy Studies, Bristol.

Shaw, M (1994) *A bibliography of family placement literature.* British Agencies for Adoption and Fostering, London.

Shaw, M, Hipgrave, T (1983) *Specialist fostering.* Batsford, London.

Shaw, M, Hipgrave, T (1989a) Specialist fostering 1988: a research report. *Adoption and Fostering* 13(3): 17–21.

Shaw, M, Hipgrave, T (1989b) Young people and their carers in specialist fostering. *Adoption and Fostering* 13(4): 11–17.

Shaw, M, Lebens, K (1977) Foster parents talking. *Adoption and Fostering* 1(2): 11–16.

Sheldon, B (1986) Social work effectiveness experiments. *British Journal of Social Work* 16: 223–242.

Shireman, J, Johnson, P (1986) A longitudinal study of black adoptions. *Social Work* May–June: 172-176.

Simmonds, J (2001) *First steps in becoming an adoptive parent: an evaluation of National Adoption Week 1999.* BAAF Adoption and Fostering, London.

Sinclair, I, Wilson, K, Gibbs, I (2000) *Supporting foster placements.* http://www.york.ac.uk/inst/swrdu/projects/fosterplacements

Small, J (1986) Transracial placements: conflicts and contradictions. In Ahmed, S, Cheetham, J, Small, J (eds) *Social work with black children and their families.* Batsford, London.

Southon, V (1986) *Children in care: paying their new families.* HMSO, London.

Stalker, K (1990) *Share the care: an evaluation of a family based respite care service.* Jessica Kingsley Publishers, London.

Stein, M (1997) *What works in leaving care?* Barnardo's, Barkingside.

Stein, TJ, Gambrill, ED, Wiltse, KT (1978) *Children in foster homes: achieving continuity of care*. Praeger, New York.

Stone, J (1991) The tangled web of short-term foster care: unravelling the strands. *Adoption and Fostering* 15(3): 4–9.

Stone, J (1995) *Making positive moves: developing short-term fostering services*. British Agencies for Adoption and Fostering, London.

Sykes, J, Sinclair, I, Gibbs, I, Wilson, K (2002) Kinship and stranger foster carers: how do they compare? *Adoption and Fostering* 26(3): 28–38.

Tesa, MF, Slack, KS (2002) The gift of kinship foster care. *Children and Youth Services Review* 24(1/2) (January/February): 79–108.

Thoburn, J (1980) *Captive clients*. Routledge, London.

Thoburn, J (1990) *Success and failure in permanent family placement*. Gower/Avebury, Aldershot.

Thoburn, J (1991) Permanent family placement and the Children Act 1989: implications for foster carers and social workers. *Adoption and Fostering* 15(3): 15–20.

Thoburn, J (1994a) *Child placement: principles and practice*. Arena, Aldershot.

Thoburn, J (1994b) The use and abuse of research in child care proceedings. In Ryburn, M (ed) *Contested adoptions: research, law, policy and practice*. Arena, Aldershot.

Thoburn, J (1996) Psychological parenting and child placement. In Howe, D (ed) *Attachment and loss in child and family social work*. Avebury, Aldershot.

Thoburn, J (2002a) *Making research count. Quality Protects research briefing 5: adoption and permanence for children who cannot live safely with birth parents or relatives*. Department of Health and Dartington Research Unit, London and Dartington.

Thoburn, J (2002b) Out of home care for the abused or neglected child: research, planning and practice. In James, A, Wilson, K (eds) *Child abuse: a reader for practitioners* (2nd edn). Ballière Tindall, Edinburgh.

Thoburn, J, Rowe, J (1991) Evaluating placements, and survey findings and conclusions. In Fratter, J, Rowe, J, Sapsford, D, Thoburn, J *Permanent family placement: a decade of experience*. British Agencies for Adoption and Fostering, London.

Thoburn, J, Murdoch, A, O'Brien, A (1986) *Permanence in child care*. Basil Blackwell, Oxford.

Thoburn, J, Norford, E, Rashid, S (2000) *Permanent family placement for children of minority ethnic origin.* Jessica Kingsley Publishers, London.

Thomas, C, Beckford, V, with Murch, M, Lowe, N (1999) *Adopted children speaking.* British Agencies for Adoption and Fostering, London.

Thorpe, R (1980) The experience of parents and children living apart. In Triseliotis, JP (ed) *New developments in foster care and adoption.* Routledge, London.

Timms, JE, Thoburn, J (2003) *Your shout! A survey of the views of 706 children and young people in public care.* National Society for the Prevention of Cruelty to Children, London.

Tizard, B (1977) *Adoption: a second chance.* Open Books, London.

Tizard, B, Hodges, J (1990) Ex-institutional children: a follow-up study to age 16. *Adoption and Fostering* 14(1): 17–20.

Trent, J (1989) *Homeward bound: the rehabilitation of children to their birth parents.* Barnardo's New Families Project, Colchester.

Trent, J (1995) Personal communication. Barnardo's New Families Project, Colchester, 20 November.

Triseliotis, J (ed) (1988) *Groupwork in adoption and foster care.* Batsford, London.

Triseliotis, J (1989) Foster care outcomes: a review of key research findings. *Adoption and Fostering* 13(3): 5–17.

Triseliotis, J (1991) *Report to the Scottish Office on the outcome of permanent family placements in two Scottish local authorities.* Scottish Office, Edinburgh.

Triseliotis, J (2002) Long-term foster care or adoption? The evidence examined. *Child and Family Social Work* 7: 23–33.

Triseliotis, JP, Russell, J (1984) *Hard to place – the outcome of adoption and residential care.* Gower, Aldershot.

Triseliotis, J, Borland, M, Hill, M (2000) *Delivering foster care.* British Agencies for Adoption and Fostering, London.

Triseliotis, J, Sellick, C, Short, R (1995) *Foster care: theory and practice.* Batsford, London.

Triseliotis, J, Shireman, J, Hundleby, M (1997) *Adoption: theory, policy and practice.* Cassell, London.

Tunnard, J, Morris, K (1996) (eds) *Messages from UK practice and research*. Family Rights Group, London.

Utting, W (1997) *People like us. The report of the review of the safeguards for children living away from home*. The Stationery Office, London.

Utting, D, Vennard, J (2000) *What works with young offenders in the community?* Barnardo's, Barkingside.

Verity, P, Nixon, S (1995) Allegations against foster families. Survey results. *Foster Care* 83 (October): 13–16.

Verity, P, Nixon, S (1996) Allegations against foster families. *Foster Care* 84 (January): 11–14.

Vernon, J, Fruin, D (1985) *In care: a study of social work decision making*. Natioinal Children's Bureau, London.

Walby, D, Symons, B (1990) *Who am I? Identity, adoption and human fertilisation*. British Agencies for Adoption and Fostering, London.

Walker, M, Hill, M, Triseliotis, J, (2002) *Testing the limits of fostering care, fostering as an alternative to secure accommodation*. BAAF Adoption and Fostering, London.

Ward, H (ed) (1995) *Looking after children: research into practice*. HMSO, London.

Waterhouse, S (1992) How foster carers view contact. *Adoption and Fostering* 16(2): 42–47.

Waterhouse, S (1997) *The organisation of fostering services: a study of the arrangements for delivering foster care services in England*. National Foster Care Association, London.

Webb, S, Aldgate, J (1991) Using respite care to prevent long-term family breakdown. *Adoption and Fostering* 15(1): 6–13.

Wedge, P, Mantle, G (1991) *Sibling groups in social work*. Avebury, Aldershot.

Welsh Assembly (2001) *Social services statistics*. Welsh Assembly, Cardiff.

Welsh Assembly (2002) *Improving placement choice and stability for children and young people who are looked after*. Welsh Assembly, Cardiff.

Westacott, J (1988) *Bridge to calmer waters – a study of a bridge families scheme.*, Barnardo's, Barkingside.

Wheal, A, Waldeman, J (1999) Family and friends as carers: identifying the training needs of carers and social workers. A research project and report. National Foster Care Association, London.

Wolkind, S, Kazuruk, A (1986) Hard to place: children with medical and developmental problems. In Wedge, P, Thoburn, J (eds) *Finding families for hard to place children*. British Agencies for Adoption and Fostering, London.

Yates, P (1985) Post-placement support. MSc dissertation, University of Edinburgh.

Index